All the B...
Melanie

MW00454570

8-Step Dream Business Plan

By Randy McCord

8-Step Dream Business Plan. Copyright@2020 Get You Visible Publishing

www.getyouvisible.com

All rights reserved. Printed in the United States of America and Canada. No part of this book may be used or reproduced in any manner whatsoever without written permission from the author, except in the case of brief quotations within critical articles or reviews.

Although the author and publisher have made every effort to ensure that the information in this book was correct at press time, the author and publisher do not assume and hereby disclaim any liability to any party due to these words coming from the author's own opinion based on their experiences.

Every word in this book is based on the author's own experience of their personal development journey and the outcomes with clients that they may have witnessed. Although we have made every reasonable attempt to achieve complete accuracy in the content of this book, we assume no responsibility for errors or omissions in the information in this book.

You should only use this information as you see fit at your own risk. Your life and circumstances may not be suited to these examples with what we share within these pages. The author and publisher are neither doctors nor in the position of registered authorities to give you expert advice. All we can share is what we have tested on ourselves and obtained through witnessing the changes in our lives or our clients' lives along the way.

The views and opinions expressed in this book are those of the authors and do not necessarily reflect the official policy, position or opinion of Get You Visible management, its partners or affiliates.

How you choose to use the information in this book within your own life is completely your own responsibility and own risk.

www.getyouvisible.com

ISBN: 978-1-989848-12-8

Randy McCord B.A. – Executive Business Director, National
Best Financial Network

Randy is a founder of National Best Financial Network, one of the most innovative and progressive life insurance brokerages in Canada. He is also exempt market licensed and is a private equity specialist with Pinnacle Wealth Brokers.

Randy and his National Best team are protection and investment specialists. However, Randy's personal focus is business clients, whether they are sole proprietors or incorporated businesses. His team is dedicated to assisting business owners looking for financial planning expertise.

Randy is a big believer in education. He has facilitated over 500 educational workshops and courses for Canadians in the last 20 years including:

- 'Investing in Real Estate' at Mount Royal University and the Calgary Board of Education
- 'Financial Road Map Workshops' with his colleagues at National Best

He has been an ardent investor, himself, for over 35 years and has been licensed in financial services for over 13 years. Randy is an alumnus of the University of Calgary.

Randy is a native Calgarian who resides on the river in Bowness with his wife, Phyllis, and Abby the busy border collie. He has two daughters who are all grown up.

He loves playing the guitar and singing. He is an aspiring songwriter and plans to record his own material as a retirement project.

Dedication

To Jean Leon Langlois and Sylvia Langlois for taking in a wayward 16-year-old who could eat them out of house and home and providing him with a stable 2nd family.

To Phyllis McCord who fell in love with a 26-year-old wayward musician and has managed to tough it out to this very day.

To Elizabeth and Catherine McCord who constantly teach this old dog new tricks.

To Maria Lizak for her faith in never giving up on the idea that I would be a great financial advisor and a dedicated business partner.

Finally, to Harwinder Kang whose business smarts and perennial smile are an inspiration to everyone on our team.

Table of Contents

Step 1. The 10-Year Dream... 4

Step 2. The 5-Year Vision.. 16

Step 3. The 3-Year Plan.. 31

Step 4. The 1-Year Goal 59

Step 5. The 3-Month Review 77

Step 6. The 1-Month Schedule 91

Step 7. The 1-Week Focus 103

Step 8. The 1-Day Task List 108

Your 8-Step Dream Business Plan: In Summary 118

Conclusion 119

8-Step Dream Business Plan

By Randy Dean McCord, BA

- Foreword by Maria Lizak, Founder and Executive Business Director, National Best

   "Believe in your Dreams. We mPower You to Succeed."

   – National Best

How to Get the Most Out of This Book and Achieve Your Dreams

This book lays out a clear road map to achieving your dreams. However, this road map will be helpful only if you are clear on where you are going and if you begin immediately. Ralph Waldo Emerson famously said, "The world makes way for the man who knows where he is going," and someone who doesn't know what they want, could end up anywhere. The first three chapters will encourage you to consider your 10-year life dreams, explore your 5-year vision for your business, and set minimum, target and outrageous annual goals for yourself and your business.

Immediate action is necessary in order to take the first steps towards your future dreams, and so that you can begin to live future dreams in the present. Let me explain. In her book, *The 5 Second Rule*, Mel Robbins explains the science behind using a bias toward action and an internal locus of control to overcome your brain's biological tendency toward procrastination and overthinking. She recommends adopting a starting ritual like the 5 Second Rule to trigger a new habit: count down from 5, 4, 3, 2, 1 and *go!* Do the thing that will move you towards your dreams. We have incorporated this principle into this book.

Raymond Aaron, in his book, *Double Your Income Doing What You Love*, recommends using instant gratification to overcome procrastination and achieve your dreams. "You can have anything you want right now as long as you begin having it right now in abbreviated form." Whatever you would like to be doing in 10 years' time, find a way to begin doing it *now*, even in a small way. If you dream of taking week-long vacations once-a-month, begin scheduling them now, even if the first few last only a couple of hours on a Saturday afternoon. As you go on this Saturday afternoon excursion, tell yourself "I am loving this glorious, one-week vacation that I take once-a-month." The important thing is to get in the habit of experiencing and talking about your dreams.

Take immediate action and tell a friend.

At the end of each chapter you will find specific action steps. Take immediate action by scheduling a specific time to work on the portion of your business plan associated with each step, by downloading the accompanying worksheet and by pre-answering the questions with the first thoughts that come to mind. This will ensure that you circumvent procrastination, the enemy of all successful business plans. One of the steps reminds you to tell a trusted friend or colleague about your plans to add accountability to your business plan.

Organize, Automate, Delegate!

Use this book to get organized. Following along with each of the 8 steps represents a part of what is needed in a complete business plan by taking you from the overall dream for your life and vision for how your business will support those dreams, to the monthly schedule, weekly focus and daily task list that will empower you to achieve those dreams.

As you are getting organized, consider what you can automate in your business. Ask yourself what tasks you (or your employees) do on a regular basis that could be systematized or even automated. Some examples in the financial services industry include: follow up confirmations emailed to the client after trades have been completed, automatic reminders for annual reviews, client birthdays and term life insurance policies coming up for renewal. Used properly, high tech solutions allow us to take a high touch, personalized approach with our clients.

2

One final piece of advice on how to get the most out of this book: as you are building or revamping your business plan, keep a running list of tasks or roles that should be delegated if they can't be automated. In order to accomplish your goals and realize your dreams, you must get to know yourself well and work with your natural talents and abilities. In his book, *What's Your Genius? How the Best THINK for Success in the New Economy*, Jay Niblick details an international study he conducted with over 197,000 people in a variety of fields to see if he could identify common factors present only among the top performers. What the study revealed is that the most successful people, labelled "geniuses" by their peers, had only two things in common: the first is that they knew well their talents and their non-talents. The second was that they ensured their success depended on their talents and not on their non-talents. In other words, these geniuses understood who they are and who they are not and invested their energy into better applying the natural talents they already possessed.

Keep this in mind when building your 8-Step Dream Business Plan. Ensure that the success of your plan depends on your natural talents. If there are tasks that are required for your success at which you are not skilled, make sure to delegate those roles to someone more skilled than you. Delegation can be accomplished by hiring employees or contractors to work in your business, or through bartering your skills with someone who has complementary skill sets in your areas of non-talent. This is the philosophy behind our *"Together, we are the best!"* tagline at National Best. When each of us focusses on working in our own areas of talent and we coordinate our efforts with others who are also working in their own areas of talent, we truly are the best.

Step 1. The 10-Year Dream

"You gotta have a dream. If you don't have a dream, how you gonna make a dream come true?" - *Oscar Hammerstein II*

All humans dream.

We have waking dreams, deep subconscious dreams while sleeping, and we have conscious dreams that reflect our future desires.

In Ancient Rome, dreams were thought to predict the future. Dream interpreters were highly sought after. Emperor Augustus had an aide force him to leave an encampment because of a dream, only to have the dream prove valuable when the camp was overrun, and the tent destroyed. After that experience, Augustus had his dreams interpreted regularly.

In modern psychology, dreams have come to represent our unconscious thoughts and desires as well as a method of interpreting life events and making sense of the cacophony of input that bombards us daily. There are even dream dictionaries to help us interpret our nightly neural wanderings. But many modern neuroscientists believe that dreams, themselves, have no meaning - they are simply the mind's way of sorting out the activities of the day, getting rid of the ones that cause stress and anxiety, and keeping the ones that will generally provide us with useful memories. In other words, dreams are like a washing machine for our basket of daily memories.

Waking dreams, however, are used quite differently. One of the definitions of human intelligence is our ability to visualize a future for ourselves and others. Our ability to formulate a future in our minds sets us apart from most other species. This is the kind of dream that we might apply to our business plan.

Possibly the most inspirational dream metaphor of my generation is the famous speech by Dr. Martin Luther King in which he imagines his ideal future:

4

"I have a dream that my four little children will one day live in a nation where they will not be judged by the color of their skin but by the content of their character. I have a dream today."

Dr. King came up with a very succinct but specific vision of a future he would like to see. So, dreams seem to be an inherent part of human character. Whatever the reason, dreams are important to us.

So, if we are to start business building, should our business plan contain a dream? We think the answer is a resounding *yes*. That is why the 8-Step Dream Business Plan begins with a dream. In fact, for many entrepreneurs, the dream can become the greatest motivator. The building of a successful business, if it is not an end unto itself, is the means to the end – the path to the dream.

We have all met the serial entrepreneur. The business owner who works tirelessly to build a business only to sell it at the peak of its success, then, begin again with some new idea or business plan. These business owners seem driven by the need to succeed, but they seem to lack the necessary element to complete their quest. Often, that element is the dream. Of course, if their dream is to build more successful businesses than anyone else, then their constant business turnover is just a part of the plan.

If a dream is to be part of our business plan, what sort of dream should it be? We believe that a business dream needs to have several components to make it valuable to our plan. Here are some questions to ask yourself to help you frame your business dream:

1.   What gets me up in the morning with energy and drive?

I, personally, have not met many people who bound out of bed bright-eyed and bushy-tailed with a smile on their face and a skip in their step, ready to take on the challenges of the day. Most people I know must shake off the fogginess of sleep and perform morning rituals before they can face the bright light of day. But there *are* those few. And in those individuals, what I have seen is an almost instant energy to get things done. How do they do it? How do they get going right away in good spirits and with a drive that seems boundless? For many of them, it boils down to their dream. They have a deep desire to fulfil their dream and that provides them with a fast start every day. Of course, there are other factors that provide for this kind of energy – one of them being preparation and another being mindset, and we will delve into those subjects in more detail in a later chapter.

So, whether you start the day like an Olympic sprinter or like a zombie risen from the dead, having a dream that you think about regularly can provide excellent motivation. Your business dream should be connected to something that you are positively passionate about. Notice that we say positively passionate and not simply passionate. You can be passionate about things that are negative. For instance, you could be passionate about watching and collecting horror films. I personally have nothing against horror films, but when it comes to a passion that relates to building your business, unless you are a film critic, this interesting hobby probably does not fit the bill. For many people, passion stems from a need to serve others, particularly their family. Many people dream of providing their spouse and children with a safe and fulfilling life where they are not concerned about money and they can create a peaceful life with the freedom to choose whatever path suits them. A passion to serve others can be a great motivator if it's your business dream.

In other cases, people are moved to great passion by material objects. For instance, Jay Leno is known as an avid car collector, as is Jerry Seinfeld. One of the passions that they can indulge in after having great success in the entertainment industry is car collecting. This can be a very expensive hobby, so making it a part of a business dream sets the bar higher than a smaller, more modest dream. But even the most modest dream can provide the energy and motivation required for some business owners. As an example, it might be the dream of a business owner to set up a branch office in a different city and help to make that office successful. They have a deep passion to provide employment to people and to serve a new community. To some, this might seem like a small dream, but to the business owner it could be their driving passion. And, from a business perspective, the nice part of this passion is that if they succeed in opening the second branch it's easy to dream of branch number three, then four...

2. What is my Why?

So, how do we develop a passion for our life? For many business gurus it boils down to *'the Why'*. In a famous TED talk video by Simon Sinek, he outlines his thesis that all business building activity should start with the Why. Ask yourself why you do what you do. Or, why does your business do what it does? Most business sales are predicated on describing the features and benefits of the product or service. This is the *what* we do part of the equation, according to Sinek. People are fine with what we do, and, in most cases, they will take into account the rational arguments put forward by salespeople based on the fine details of the features or the solution gained by the benefits. But Sinek tells us that is not enough. Even if they understand *how* you do what you do, that is just information and data and does not reach into the feelings and emotions of the limbic mind where our real decision-making processes lay. People may hear your pitch, understand your product, get the benefits, and still not be interested in buying because it just does not *feel right*. People buy your product or service because they believe in your Why. In other words, they believe what you believe, and that creates trust and loyalty in your customers, in your employees and in your own mind. So, become clear on your Why and that will help you develop your passion.

3. What is my purpose?

Your Why often derives from your purpose. For spiritual folk, their purpose is a God-given gift. They believe that a supreme being has imbued them with special gifts that allow them to serve their constituents, customers and comrades, and that they were born for this purpose. It is this belief in purpose that gives them their Why. Now, not all people are spiritual in this respect. So, if you don't have a belief in a godlike entity, how can you gain insight into your own purpose? How can you then translate that purpose into a compelling Why that will drive your business plan?

One method that is used by many businesses today is to attach their services to a charitable cause. If you can think of a charity or non-profit society that you would support with 100% of your time and money if you were able, then that could be a purpose to evolve your Why. Unfortunately, this activity has come to be seen by many as just another marketing scheme by large corporations. But there is still a way to achieve the creation of your Why from your need to give. Simply keep your charitable donations private but translate the need into your Why. As an example, you may wish to eradicate poverty in your city. This could be your overriding purpose. To achieve the purpose, you decide that your business should contribute to a non-profit organization dedicated to assisting the disadvantaged. You can then translate this purpose into the reason you do business, and even pass this purpose along to your employees as the overriding Why in your business. But to avoid the trap of appearing to use this Why as a marketing scheme, explain to your employees that you don't plan to advertise this activity, but if customers were to ask, they are free to outline the program. In this way, your why can grow organically throughout the organization and be communicated to your clientele without appearing self-serving.

Your organizational Why can also be purely customer related. In the financial service industry, a company might create a mission to provide specific education for its clients about a strategy or product that is often misunderstood or misrepresented. As an example, at National Best Financial, one of our Whys is to provide financial education and literacy to Canadians. This means that we will take the time to explain financial products and concepts to individuals even if they are not clients. As financial advisors, this is not a recommended strategy to quickly build a book of business. However, it gives our advisors a purpose beyond simply making money. They feel as if they have a mission to fulfill - to help their fellow citizens and, in turn, a typical prospect is made to feel that a National Best representative is not there simply to sell them a product but to provide good advice. When the Why is attached to a purpose and mission that transcends good business practice and maximizing profit, all stakeholders can feel comfortable in their day-to-day interactions. In turn, this can translate into brand building that creates a strong positive reputation.

Reputation risk is important in many industries, so if you can build a company culture that naturally builds strong positive reputation - that is a Why worth pursuing. The creation of a mission for ourselves and our employees as a means to fulfil our purpose and create our Why is essential. In the next chapter, we will discuss a mission statement which further clarifies this concept for the entire organization.

4. How big should my dream be?

A dream is like an ocean sunset. As we stand on the shore and look out at the horizon, we can see a tiny spec - an island paradise where we would love to live. It would be a magical place where there would be no need to worry about anything. We wouldn't need money, food would be abundant, and all the inhabitants would be loving and friendly. And though it is far away, we know that if we build a sturdy boat and learn to navigate, we could eventually reach our island paradise. In other words, don't settle for less than the most amazing thing you can imagine when it comes to your business dream. If it's going to be the thing that gets you revved up every day, you may as well make it a big dream.

In the beginning, most new advisors in our industry are simply looking to make a living, so their dream consists of monetary goals. As they gain experience and a broader vision of their market, their revenue expectations begin to increase, and soon they can visualize a very large monetary goal. There is nothing wrong with using wealth as the basis of a business dream. Most of us are in business for that very reason – we expect to make more money building our own business than working for a salary building someone else's.

However, many business coaches and behavioral experts point out that once most people have achieved a certain amount of income or wealth, the money begins to become less meaningful. And if there is one thing that human beings crave more than almost anything, it is a life that has meaning. Once again, this drives us back to our purpose and our Why. Although we may start with the dream of achieving wealth, inevitably the bigger dream relates to our purpose and our reason for being. For most people, this relates to service to humanity. Certainly, there are people who simply live for the sake of themselves, but the experts tell us that even the hedonists eventually tire of the good things in life if they have no one to share with. So, if we are to attach our business dream to something that will provide an ongoing solid foundation of meaning and purpose, odds are that it will work best if that dream is bent on making the world a better place for everyone. Not only can you, as the business owner, buy into a higher purpose, but it will also provide a bigger Why for your employees. No employee wants to work hard for a company that appears to only benefit the owners and the shareholders. Everyone wants to believe that in their short working life, they have made a difference.

Most of us have heard many beauty pageant contestants espouse world peace as their dream for humanity. We may think that this is just the naïve response of a young and inexperienced person, but the truth is that great big dreams help to drive our actions. A business dream that is large, all-encompassing and passionate by nature can act as a driving force for both the owner and the employees. In the small village of today's media connected world, just working for a wage has no meaning. Humanity is too impatient in the present age of instantaneous information exchange to just be satisfied with day-to-day drudgery to pay the bills. Generational differences are becoming more and more pronounced. We often hear about millennials not wanting to work at menial jobs, having no loyalty to a company and expecting all sorts of perks and bonuses regardless of their experience. That is because they dream of a different world. They are unwilling to accept the status quo when it comes to the kind of working life they would like to have. To those of us in previous generations, these attitudes can seem shallow and entitled - but perhaps we judge too quickly. The truth is, we were told these very same things decades ago as the information age began. I remember back in the '80s there was talk of a 20-hour work week and an economy filled with service jobs, since automation and robotics would be taking over all the menial and physical tasks involved in construction and manufacturing. In truth, many of those business dreams came to fulfilment, however, the shortened work week did not. In fact, many people found themselves having to work more hours to make ends meet. Big dreams that almost came true. That is surely the nature of dreams in general.

The lesson is to make your business dream a real eye-opener. Make it something that you can believe in passionately. Make it so that you can easily transfer that passion to your family, your friends, your employees, your suppliers, your clients and to the world.

Write Down Your Dream

There is power in writing stuff down. There is an old business story, most likely apocryphal, that claims there was a study at Harvard or Yale (depending on how you Google it) that showed students who wrote down their goals were ten times more successful than those who did not. And, of course, only 3% of the students wrote down their goals and they achieved more than the other 97% put together – or so goes the story. I have heard many business coaches use this story as a reason to write down goals. I highly suspect the story is an urban myth, but the fact remains that writing does help achievement – but, not for the reason most people think.

When I talk about writing something down, I mean physically writing in cursive with a pen or pencil. It is the *physical act* that makes it work. The movement of pen on paper provides us with a physical cue to aid in memory retention. Also, our own handwriting makes what is written seem more intimate and personal. This is the reason that writing down your business dream is important. In fact, I recommend that people write out their dream regularly. Don't just print it out on a piece of paper and slap it on the wall. Rather, write it out in your quarterly review, or into your monthly schedule, or at the start of your weekly target or even at the beginning of your daily task list. There is no harm in being reminded of your great big business dream regularly.

Make a Simplified Version in a few Sentences

We could write a business dream that is very detailed and paragraphs in length, but what we want is a simplified version of our dream that we can write out in a few sentences. We want to be able to easily memorize it and pass it on to others. I recommend to business owners who are not English majors like myself, to hire a content writer. The content writer can help to make the dream flow naturally and provide specific words for impact. You certainly want your business dream to be succinct and powerful.

Build a Dream Board to Hang in your Office

Words are important, but images can invoke a whole different feeling when it comes to communicating a dream. One of the best ways to represent our dream visually is to build a dream or vision board (not to be confused with a corporate vision which we will discuss in the next chapter). Often, people are introduced to a dream board via a workshop which often seems more like a crafting class or a scrapbook club than it does a serious business building exercise. To be clear, we are trying to sculpt a graphic representation of our company's dream. That means we must pick our images and our medium carefully. Just cutting out interesting photos for magazines and pasting them randomly onto construction paper is not the answer.

Before embarking on a dream board exercise it's important to think carefully about how it should be constructed, what material should be used and the kinds of images that should be sought after. Also, consider making copies. The dream board should not be hidden away at the back of the office; it should have a prominent role wherever there is executive, employee or client traffic. Therefore, care must be taken in its construction. It needs to spark people's imagination when they think about your corporate brand and your long-term purpose. It should be a carefully constructed collage that invokes an inspirational message.

Post it Everywhere

So, post it everywhere. When you finally have a perfectly crafted dream board make sure that everyone involved in your company is aware of the destination. Make sure you don't mix up the dream board with your corporate branding. Corporate brands should be easily accessible and relatively simple by comparison. Of course, there may be examples of your brand, including logos, incorporated into the dream board. But, typically, we are not using the dream board for branding purposes, we are using it to visually depict our purpose.

Talk About Your Dream Unashamedly to your Friends and Colleagues

Don't keep your dream a secret - chat about it with your friends, share it with everyone. Bring it up with your colleagues and business partners on a regular basis. Even let your clients in on the dream so that they can feel that they're a part of something more than simply purchasing services. Your corporate or business dream needs to be disseminated as widely as possible.

Beginning every working day with the idea that you're getting one step closer to one of your life's most important landmarks is key to keeping you motivated and on track. One of the hardest lessons for most financial advisors is to embrace rejection. Rejection will show up in many forms. You will be rejected by potential clients. You will have applications rejected by underwriters. You will have claims that are rejected, marketing material that is rejected by compliance, and applications and trades that are rejected due to missing information, miscommunication and mismanagement. Remaining positive in the face of this headwind of constant negative feedback is the key to long-term success in your business. The trick to staying positive is to review your dream daily. No matter the challenges of yesterday, the first thought of a new day should be: *what great things shall befall me today that will lead me closer to my dream?*

So, why make it a 10-year dream? Why not a 7-year dream, or a 15-year dream? The truth is that the timeline is not the most important feature. The only reason I chose a 10-year dream for the 8-Step Dream Business Plan was because most financial advisors reach a significant level of success and competency by their tenth year in business. If they can survive the first two or three years of struggle, they begin to find their business feet. They start to define a market and perhaps a specialty. They begin to accept certain industry norms and are not as intimidated by the regulations and bureaucracies that pervade financial services. In 10 years, a typical financial advisor can build a solid book of business that can often sustain their family and provide a consistent cash flow. Once that benchmark has been met, they are free to explore building their practice as they see fit, or as befits their dream. They can now begin to visualize the dream more clearly or, perhaps, they have even fulfilled their business dream so now they can broaden their dream to encompass new goals. My personal 10-year dream is still far from fruition after over a decade in the business, but that's okay. I can't swim to my island paradise yet, but I can see the trees and some of the landmarks. I just need to trim my sails and catch the right breeze and I will be there in no time.

However, if a 10-year dream does not work for your business model, then by all means, adjust the timeline. Some business owners want to build their business for 5 years and then sell it off. They might have a 5-year dream. Others might want to build a practice that will service their community for the next 20 years, so they might have a 25-year dream.

What about multiple dreams? We touched on this earlier. There is no reason not to have a variety of dreams if they serve your business building. Just remember, your dream is not your corporate vision or mission - we will discuss those in the next chapter. Keep your dream big and beautiful and make it a long stretch to get there.

Immediate Action Steps:
- Book a time in your calendar in the next week or two to do some dreaming. Ensure you will have at least an hour of uninterrupted time. Use your favorite location in your house or neighborhood,

if you are used to dreaming there, or pick a new location with a beautiful view in order to inspire you to greater things. *Do it now.*

- Text or email a trusted friend or colleague about your intention to spend this time dreaming. *Do it now.*

- Write down a couple of ideas or images that came to mind when reading this chapter. This will help you get started with your dreaming session. You might write a note in a new notebook or journal or type a note in the Word document available for download or dictate an audio note. *Do it now.*

- Begin collecting images for your dream board. Open an internet search and save some images on your desktop or on your smart phone, start a new Pinterest search and pin pictures that capture what you would like to do, be and have in 10-years' time. *Do it now.*

Step 2. The 5-Year Vision

"Vision without action is merely a dream. Action without vision just passes the time. Vision with action can change the world."
- Joel A. Barker

The quote above by the famous business author and futurist, Joel A. Barker, explains why just having a dream for your business is not enough. Our dream may drive our purpose. It may provide us with the motivation to keep going when we hit ruts in the road. But it is not enough to provide us with a detailed picture of our business that will allow us to take specific action in pursuit of that end.

It is our vision that provides us with the detailed characteristics of the business we wish to build. Our dream may be pie-in-the-sky, but our vision is very much grounded. Our dream may be a barely visible island on the horizon, but our vision contains all the details of our paradise. Our vision sees the sandy beaches and the clear blue ocean. It details the palm trees, the trickling streams, the mouth-watering fruit and the abundance of tropical wildlife that inhabits our island. In the same way, our business vision outlines our business paradise, giving us enough detail to allow us to act with intention. As Mr. Barker says, action without vision is aimless. But when we have a vision, and we direct our actions toward achieving that vision, then we have clear intention in all of the things that we do to build our business.

Not everyone is a visionary. Most entrepreneurs trying to build a business have some kind of vision in mind, but not everyone is a visionary in the way that Bill Gates, Steve Jobs or Richard Branson turned out to be. Many of us simply want to build a comfortable living. In fact, when most financial advisors begin their career, their primary goal is putting food on the table. This necessity does not leave much room for visionary exercises. However, no matter how we started in business we must have some idea of where we are going. So, even if you are not a great dreamer or don't have big visions of your future business, it does not mean that you cannot construct a vision to help focus your efforts.

The 5-year vision is meant to focus activity toward a business goal. What that means is that your vision is malleable and can change over time; particularly as the financial advisor begins to grow as a specialist and better understands the opportunities available in the industry and in the marketplace.

In the beginning, their vision might be quite modest. They might simply be looking for a comfortable living for themselves and their family. As they move through the process of learning about their industry, they may find niche markets, products and strategies that excite them, certain kinds of clients about whom they are very passionate and other important information that will lead them to expand or alter their original vision. This is a natural process. The important thing is to have a vision that allows you to zero-in on activities that are going to be productive every day. A vision is there as a step toward the dream. Although we mentioned visualizing and building a big dream, our vision should be considered one of the steps toward achieving the dream. What this means is that as we move through our business process, if it becomes clear that our vision is not in tune and in step with our dream, then we must do one of two things:

1. change our dream, or

2. change our vision

Today, many business coaches talk about a lack of congruence to describe this type of conflict. If our dream, our vision and our actions are all moving in the same direction – congruent - then great things can be achieved. When there is no congruence, chaos can result.

I have seen lack of congruence many times in our industry. Some financial services companies recruit advisors based on a 'big dream'. They use the dream just as we have described in the previous chapter – trying to motivate the new recruit to massive action in order to build an income.

Unfortunately, it is the company's dream – not the individual's dream - that is being constantly reinforced. This can lead the recruit to believe that if they just keep going, no matter what, they will achieve success. That can be a true statement in our business if you can survive. But you can burn a lot of time, money and relationships if you are not careful. I have seen advisors lose all their savings, many of their friends and even their spouse over their single-minded devotion to a leadership that was not working in their best interest.

Less than 10% of advisors who enter our industry ever make a great living and even less build a big business. In fact, most financial services companies who recruit responsibly require new recruits to take a famous test, decades old, called the POP Quiz (found at https://www.selfmgmt.com/). It was developed to help determine if a new recruit is suitable for our industry. Green means go, yellow means coaching required and red means keep your day job. If you are being recruited to an organization based on a dream, then ask what kind of criteria they use to determine your suitability for the position. If there is none, then perhaps there is a different agenda at work. Maybe you are being recruited to work for someone else's dream.

We can often lose sight of reality if we get too attached to a dream without the requisite components to complete the plan. That is why vision and mission are so important as we flesh out our plan.

When we started National Best, we wanted to build a new model – something different that had never been seen in our industry. Our founders sat down and started to work out what that business model and vision would look like. I am the first to admit that I was not one of the visionaries. That is not my natural skill set. One of my colleagues often refers to me as her General, which means I am an implementer of action, but I'm not particularly interested in trying to develop some broad vision and detailed business model. I am happy to provide input and act as an editor for the business but coming up with the original ideas was the work of a couple of our visionary founders. However, this did not stop me from developing a vision for my own business. Remember, the vision I have for my business can be different from the overall vision of my company. This is particularly true in financial services.

As an example, a financial advisor may be working for a large publicly traded corporation that has very different goals in mind and a very different vision for the next five years than the individual advisor. The advisor may be looking to build a book of 250 clients, whereas the company may be looking to increase shareholder value and prepare themselves for a merger. In some cases, these visions may work in concert whereas in other cases they may conflict with one another. Therefore, it's quite important, as an individual business builder, that we make sure that our affiliates, our partners, and our colleagues clearly understand our vision and how it fits into the overall goals of our plan – and that their plans do not conflict with ours in a way that creates a total incongruence of purpose.

In many companies today, you will see a vision statement on the wall, in the hallway or at the entrance to their office. The idea of a vision has become very popular. The reason for this is that the statement focuses action.

Here are some samples of famous vision statements:

Oxfam
A just world without poverty.

Ikea
To create a better everyday life for the many people.

Microsoft
Empower every person and every organization on the planet to achieve more.

Nike
Bring inspiration and innovation to every athlete* in the world. (*If you have a body, you are an athlete).

Ford
People working together as a lean, global enterprise to make people's lives better through automotive and mobility leadership.

Avon
To be the company that best understands and satisfies the product, service and self-fulfillment needs of women—globally.

Apple
To produce high-quality, low cost, easy to use products that incorporate high technology for the individual.

Tesla
To accelerate the world's transition to sustainable energy.

Chevron
At the heart of The Chevron Way is our Vision to be the global energy company most admired for its people, partnership and performance.

Coca-Cola
To achieve sustainable growth, we have established a vision with clear goals.
Profit: Maximizing return to shareowners while being mindful of our overall responsibilities.

People: Being a great place to work where people are inspired to be the best they can be.

Portfolio: Bringing to the world a portfolio of beverage brands that anticipate and satisfy people's desires and needs.

Partners: Nurturing a winning network of partners and building mutual loyalty.

Planet: Being a responsible global citizen that makes a difference.

The Components of a Great Vision Statement

What makes a great vision statement?

Notice that although all the companies above are trying to describe a future event or outcome, their vision statements are generally written in the present tense. Most business gurus will agree with this protocol. The argument usually goes something like this: our unconscious minds don't perceive time so a statement that becomes unconsciously implanted can become manifested in the brain even if it hasn't happened yet. In other words, a statement in the present tense tricks our unconscious brain into believing that it has already happened. I personally am not a big believer in these sorts of mind game gymnastics; however, I don't see any harm in assembling a vision statement in the present tense to imply a desired outcome. Most of the examples above represent a summarized phrase. Many of these companies and organizations have fully fleshed out visions that might be paragraphs, or even pages, long. Again, there is nothing wrong with having a clearly delineated vision. But in order to make it memorable to yourself, your employees, your colleagues and your partners, it's important that the summarized phrase be direct and powerful. It should do its best to sum up the 5-Year Vision and to describe it in a way that allows us to feel a part of the direction, the value system, and the intent of a growing organization.

Harwinder Kang, the president of National Best Financial Network and a successful businessman in other areas of the Calgary business community, often would quote the vision statement of the oil and gas company to whom he was employed for many years as an engineer. He said that it stuck with him because it encompassed all of the goals he thought the company was meant to achieve and that he could be a part of. That's the kind of statement that we are looking for in our 5-Year Vision.

A great vision statement should evoke emotion as much as it describes the future outcome of our business activities. It needs to stir us up, while remaining direct and simple. When creating a vision statement, we should avoid the use of numbers that could prove limiting and any kind of business speak that could be misinterpreted. In short, a company's vision statement is best when it can paint a clear picture of a future that includes company values, a common purpose, a passionate cause and the definition of success.

The 5-Year Vision should be a big picture statement clearly outlining what the organization should look like and the relevance that it has to the organizational team and its clients. We are asking our employees to be inspired by the statement - thus the need for it to be memorable, yet simple. Because we want the statement to inspire, it needs to be relevant to all stakeholders, specific enough for people to grasp onto it easily and it must be purposeful in that it should have a clear direction that is easily understood. To the extent that the company has not achieved this vision yet, it should throw down the gauntlet and challenge employees, management, ownership and other direct stakeholders to achieve the higher standards embodied by the vision statement.

In order to fully describe our 5-Year Vision we may find that one statement is not enough. Even our expanded vision, the one that goes beyond our succinct summary, may not be able to fully encapsulate all our stakeholders. As an example, when the leadership at National Best Financial Network were working on our vision statement, we found that it made sense to have an internal vision statement as well as an external vision statement. Our internal statement was meant for our advisors and employees, whereas our external statement was meant to relay our corporate vision to our clients, our suppliers and other collaborators. Here is our summary, or internal vision statement:

nbVISION

To Build a Strong NETWORK **of Independent Financial Professionals Connected by a Collaborative Culture**

Together we are the **Best!**

*m*Powered by

And here is the expanded, external statement:

TOGETHER – When we each focus on what we do best...

TOGETHER, we are the BEST!

WE'VE ALL GOT A PIECE OF THE PUZZLE – It is important for each of us to know what our talents are, and what they are not. When we work in our area of talent, and coordinate our efforts with others who are working in their own areas of talent, we truly are the best.

NATIONAL BEST BUSINESS NETWORK – NBBN is a network of independent Advisors and Agencies that use their areas of specialty to serve our clients' needs for:

- *Debt and Cashflow Solutions*

- *Insurance Solutions*

- *Investment Solutions*

- *Estate Planning Solutions*

23

TOGETHER, we are the BEST!

You can see that our summary statement relates primarily to our own internal business processes whereas the expanded, or external statement goes on to include the important services we provide to our clients. This makes the overall vision statement inclusive of more stakeholders, however, it is the summary statement that is hanging on the wall in the office. Our goal as a company is to maintain a strict model of independence for our advisors, levering that independence into honest advice for our clients. When we make the bold claim to be the *best,* we are careful to add the motto that we use as a branding tagline – *Together, We Are the Best.* This combination of vision statement and tagline work perfectly together to explain how we can work as independent advisors and yet provide a higher level and more comprehensive experience to our clients.

I would like to look at the 5-Year Vision in a different way. I would like to take the perspective of the individual advisor. At the end of the day, in the independent model of financial services, each of us is running our own business. It is true that I passionately buy into the vision of my company, but does that vision apply directly to my own book of business and my own local agency? To the extent that I want to expand the message of professionalism and collaboration, it does apply. But when it comes to my own personal goals, the corporate vision is too broad. It does not create a specific enough picture for my personal 5-Year Vision. That's why I always recommend that advisors come up with their own personal vision statement. The company vision statement can be proudly hung in the hallway of your office, but your personal vision statement can be taped onto your bathroom mirror alongside your 10-Year Dream. There is nothing more powerful than a combination of big dream, specific vision and a plan to get there. In the next chapter we are going to zero-in on that 3-Year Plan. In the meantime, here are some interesting questions to ask about your personal vision statement:

- What can you see on the horizon in the next 5 years?

- What will your business look like?

- What will the numbers look like?

- How many clients will you have?

- What will your personal income be?

- What will the income of your partners & employees be?

- How long should my vision statement be?

Post It Where You Will See It Every Day.

What is my Mission (How do I get to my Vision)?

Notice that for a personal vision statement I am not avoiding things like specific numbers as suggested for the company vision statement. That's because our personal vision statement is a lot closer to home. Our personal 5-Year Vision might be very income specific since it could be tied to a monetary goal such as purchasing a home, purchasing a cottage or preparing for retirement. In this case, we want our directed activity, our intentional purpose, to keep us on track for these personal targets.

Here is my earliest vision statement when I first formulated the 8-Step Dream Business Plan:

> In 5 years, I will have an *nb*Agency with 10 full-time advisors who will generate a total of $1 Million in annual commission. I will generate $250,000.00 in personal production annually.

Have I achieved this vision? Not yet. But it remains as a reminder of the kind of agency I would like to have. Whether it happens in the next few years, in the next five years or even in the next 10 years, it is a specific and accurate statement of what I would like my business to be.

Before we leave our chapter on the 5-Year Vision, we need to talk about one other statement that almost always accompanies the vision statement – the mission statement. These two statements are inextricably linked - we need a vision to help direct our actions and we need a mission to tell us how to get there. Our 5-Year vision is what we want our business to look like in the future and our mission represents the means by which we will get there.

Here are some powerful mission statements:

"To connect the world's professionals to make them more productive and successful."

"To enrich people's lives with programmes and services that inform, educate and entertain."

"To organize the world's information and make it universally accessible and useful."

You can see that these mission statements explain how the company is going to achieve its goal, but not what it's going to look like five years hence. This is the true difference between a mission statement and a vision statement. The vision is the *what*, and the mission is the *how*. I have always felt more comfortable sculpting mission statements because, as I've mentioned, I felt my skills were better directed to implementation programs rather than visionary activities. I'm the fellow who always says: "if you're going to tell me about the great thing you did, please tell me how you did it." There is nothing more frustrating to a student of business than to have some guru show off a highly successful client yet provide absolutely no detail on how that client achieved their vision. It is somewhat like doing a jigsaw puzzle. You can see the finished product on the box cover but achieving that lovely picture is a slow, tedious process that would go much faster if parts of the puzzle were already finished.

A clear, precise mission statement is the key to our day-to-day activities. Our mission statement keeps us focused on the *how* - in other words, it informs our weekly target and our daily task list.

The National Best Mission statement is an excellent example.

*nb*Mission

- We *mPower*™ Advisors and Agencies to build productive, profitable businesses, improving the financial future of Canadians.

- We *mPower*™ Clients to take control of their financial futures by providing solutions to manage debt and improve cash flow, protect income and assets, retire with dignity and live their dreams.

Believe in Your Dreams!
We mPower™ *You to Succeed!*

mPowered by

*nb*Mission

Through education, practical application of knowledge, relationships, accountability, networking and mentoring we help people to fulfill their purpose and passion:

Believe in Your Dreams!
We mPower™ *You to Succeed!*

mPowered by

Notice that we have split our mission statement into two types, one inclusive of both advisors and clients, and the other very client specific. This is so we can keep our eye on the prize, which is providing our clients with the best service possible in our collaborative model. The first version is meant to be used internally, whereas the second version can be shared with the client. Notice that the client version does not specify the kinds of services we provide, but rather draws on emotional cues to describe our mission. We are not just in the protection and wealth creation business. Ultimately, we want our clients to fulfill their dreams and desires. If they achieve their goals, then we are all successful. We try to instill hope in the client that their dreams are not out of reach if we plan carefully and execute well.

Here is my personal mission statement:

> **To provide exemplary risk management and investment services to Canadian business owners and families, based on the highest level of ethics and empathy in our industry.**

My mission statement relates much more directly to my own market direction and business goals. In fact, that is the aim of The 8-Step Dream Business Plan. It represents a business plan that is more personal and was originally developed to assist individual financial advisors. However, much of the structure of the 8-Step Dream Business Plan can also be used for team building or corporate planning.

To summarize, vision statements allow us to more clearly define our 5-year goals and provide a step toward our 10-year dream. Our mission statement defines our fundamental basis for action. The combination of the two can provide powerful motivation and clear direction. We should be able to share our vision and mission statements with our colleagues and clients, but we may also have personal definitions that relate to our individual goals.

Immediate Action Steps:

- Book a time in your calendar in the next several weeks to write down your vision and mission for your business. Ensure you will have at least an hour of uninterrupted time. This may be scheduled at the same time as your dreaming session, or a week or two later, marking the beginning of habitual business-planning sessions that you schedule. You will want to ensure that you have your dream board with you to inspire you. *Do it now.*

- Text or email a trusted friend or colleague about your intention to spend this time creating your vision and mission for your business. *Do it now.*

- Download the vision worksheet and save it to your device. Have a quick look at the vision questions (also listed in the chapter above) and write down any answers that come to mind. This will help you get started with a vision writing session. *Do it now.* https://mailchi.mp/93c0d198a165/8-step-dream-business-plan-worksheet

Step 3. The 3-Year Plan

"To achieve great things, two things are needed; a plan, and not quite enough time."

— *Leonard Bernstein, composer and conductor*

When I was in school, many years ago, my favorite classes were history and social studies. I loved to hear about ancient civilizations, stories of great empires, the causes and outcomes of great wars and battles and how that knowledge could help us understand the study of modern societies. I remember one year we spent all semester studying Russia. Since they were the only country in the world that was bigger than Canada, and they had the only hockey team that could compete with us, most Canadians were interested in Russian society. Of course, those were the USSR years and we in the West were very derisive of their communist system of government.

But one area where their government seemed to carry some credence was their ability to plan. We were taught about Stalin's famous 5-year plan. After the second world war, in an attempt to rebuild the country, Stalin had his bureaucrats prepare plans for reconstruction and they were based around the idea that a project could be complete within a five-year time span. In the West, many of our governments were elected every four years so it was virtually impossible for a government to make plans on a five-year basis. Only massive infrastructure projects were typically planned and funded on that basis and they were generally considered a necessity and superseded political interests. But in Russia, the totalitarian regime could simply make the decision, formulate the plan, implement the plan and move ahead toward their goal. Of course, today we know that although the plans may have looked good on paper, the bureaucracy and political intrigue within the Russian regime often prevented projects from coming to fruition or even beginning at all. Essentially, plans only work if they are fully implemented. And even the best laid plans rarely work perfectly. If we wait until we think we have the perfect plan, then we have usually waited too long. Or, as George S. Patton once said:

"A good plan violently executed now is better than a perfect plan executed next week."

What he is saying is that no plan is perfect. Action supersedes any flaws the plan may have. In fact, there is no way to test to see if the plan is perfect unless it is implemented, and the work begins. This means that plans are not written in stone. They are living, malleable documents and should be treated as such. Gen. Patton's old boss, Dwight D. Eisenhower, had another famous quote about planning:

"Plans are nothing; planning is everything."

Any plan is in a constant state of change. It is the planning itself that provides us with our direction forward. Once the plan is formulated and the command is set to commence, we might as well burn it. This is because as soon as we analyze feedback with regard to our plan, it will inevitably instruct us to alter it.

But the plan is still the plan. We still need to write down and document something which will provide us with the direction to fulfil our vision.

So, why a 3-Year Plan? Why not the 5-year plan that seemed to work so well for post-war Russia? Well, times have changed, and the world moves at a much faster pace than it did back then. Consider the semi-conductor industry. This industry has doubled in performance and capacity at a tremendous rate since the '60s. Although Gordon Moore, former CEO of Intel, predicted a doubling of computer performance capacity every two years back in 1965, he considered that it would continue for about 10 years. Not only was he correct about the doubling, but it continued for decades - thus coining the term *Moore's Law*. This is just one example of the speed of current change. Information and data exchange have also sped up with the growth of computing capacity. Keeping business secrets and plans private is becoming more and more difficult and complex. So, trying to plan for a 5-year implementation process does not seem realistic anymore. What we know and believe today about our business environment could be completely turned around in five years. Most tech startups today work around a 3-Year Plan from conception to launch. If it takes them any longer to go to market, they risk being left in the dust by their competitors.

Even the 3-Year Plan might be a bit of a stretch in today's volatile business environment. However, three years provides us with a big enough planning canvas to paint a long-term picture of the kind of business activities that will accomplish our vision and, ultimately, our 10-Year Dream.

So, how do we go about starting our 3-Year Plan?

Most businesses, in the end, are dependent upon numbers. We need to calculate all the factors that play into how we can produce revenue and, ultimately, how much of that revenue sustains and grows our business. And unlike dreams and visions, the numbers inside of our 3-Year Plan represent the reality of our business life. The numbers won't lie. They will reveal to us the hard facts about our plans.

This is one of the reasons that, when I spoke about a personal vision, I included revenue numbers as a goal. Without the gross revenue numbers, we really don't have a measurable target. It is one thing to see the island of our dreams on the horizon, but it is quite another to navigate to it successfully. The numbers will give us our coordinates and help us plot a course.

There are a couple of ways to look at the issue of revenue projection. We can see it as an annual event (which is part of our 1-Year Goal section), but when it comes to our 5-Year Vision and 3-Year Plan, we need to think strategically. Does it make sense to take the total and just divide by five years? That would mean that we would have to get off to a tremendous start and then maintain that pace with no growth for the term of the plan. This approach, typically, does not make sense. For most businesses, and certainly for most financial advisors who are at the outset of their career, there is a period of slow growth as our plans are formulated and implemented. Unless a product or service has a natural untapped market with little or no competition, growth will be incremental as the business steps into the marketplace and tries to make an impact via marketing and sales. And once we have the numbers figured out, we can start making viable marketing and sales decisions.

Reverse Engineer the Numbers Needed to Reach the Vision

The first step in our 3-Year Plan is to figure out target revenue. For larger businesses this could mean running at a loss for the first year or two, especially a startup with a new product. In some cases, tech startups can run at a loss for years and we often see them go public with huge valuations before they have ever turned a profit. That is okay for a large global entity, but for your personal plan, well, we need to pay the bills month to month, so a personal 3 -Year Plan should try not to subsidize the first years' operation. Again, we will go into more detail in our 1-Year Goal section, but suffice it to say that our first-year revenue should, at least, pay our bills. In other words, we are looking for at least a minimum level of production that can sustain a basic lifestyle.

Once we have established our minimum revenue goal, we can then proceed to make some growth assumptions that can allow us to build our business in order to reach our 5-Year Vision numbers. We might decide that we can produce 20% growth every year. Our 3-Year Plan then needs to contain the elements that will drive us to those results. Or, it may be that we see a more exponential growth pattern. Perhaps 10%, 20%, 30% in the first three years. If we do not have any historical data from which to make projections, then we must break down production in different ways. So, for a startup advisor, they should lean on their compatriots in the industry to find out what the average production numbers look like and where they can find data to support their plan. As an example, a review of an advisor who produces $100,000 in annual revenue might contain data indicating that 50% of his business came from referrals and 50% derived from other marketing efforts including retirement seminars and financial planning workshops. Drilling down further into the data might show that of the referral business, 40% came from current clients, 40% from networking business groups and 20% from other external referral sources. Of the revenue from seminars and workshops, we might discover that 80% of that revenue came from lunch & learns at companies where the advisor was providing group benefit plans. Deeper analysis can show us even more detail about these various marketing strategies. This data provides the new advisor with some idea of what to expect, should he embark on a similar business model.

On the other hand, our newbie might run into an advisor who is a cold call expert. They might be able to show data that breaks down sales calls into usable tables. For instance, we might discover that this advisor was also able to produce $100,000 in annual revenue but he did it almost entirely by getting on the telephone and calling potential customers. The numbers might look something like this: 25 daily calls netted 5 appointments, which in turn produced 1 new client. If that average could be reproduced by a new advisor, then they could expect similar results in their first year. However, our experience tells us this is not usually the case, since our newbie must collect names and contact info and the initial startup might hamper their efficiency in the beginning. Also, they will have to sculpt a script that feels comfortable and natural, and, most importantly, they will have to learn about the power of hearing the word *no*, repeatedly. If these issues seem too daunting to our new advisor, then they may have to look for other marketing plans to fill out their 3-Year Plan. Everyone is different when it comes to the marketing and sales process. Finding the perfect marketing strategy for your business may mean trying a few different options until you find some success and can build on that platform.

Marketing always precedes sales in any business plan. So, as a part of our 3-Year Plan revenue projection, we should include the costs for whatever marketing process we put in place. A new advisor with a very modest budget might have to resort to cold calls. A business who wished to reach out on social media may spend money on a website, landing pages and content for a social media campaign on Facebook, Twitter, LinkedIn, Instagram etc. In either case, there will be a budget. That budget number should be worked into the minimum projections for the 3-Year Plan. It may be that we plan to revisit old contacts in a previous industry, and we will invite them out for coffee or lunch. If so, then the costs for these activities should be included in our projected numbers. Lunches and coffees can add up quickly. Keeping an eye on these costs from the beginning will help a new business conserve working capital. Also, it is vital to keep track of the return on investment for these activities. It makes no sense to continue to wine and dine your potential clients or referral partners if they are sending you no business. We will look more carefully at tracking our numbers when we get to our chapter on the 3-Month Review.

Business plan templates are available in great number on the internet. In Alberta, a great source of free business information is the Business Link, a government sponsored organization whose mandate is to assist Alberta entrepreneurs and companies to prepare for launch and growth. I recommend checking out their website at www.businesslink.ca. They have a template for a business plan that includes the common sections you'll find in most business plans. These sections include:

- Executive Summary
- Risk and Mitigation
- Promotion/Marketing
- Business Background
- Industry/Market Analysis
- Management
- Operations
- Environmental Issues
- Financial Projections and Analysis
- Opportunities for Growth
- Exit Strategies
- References
- Appendices

One interesting aspect of the Business Link list is the lack of a sales category. That seems strange since, for most businesses, it is sales that will drive revenue. In this case, the list encompasses the sales process within some of the other categories – operations and marketing, for instance. I prefer a separate category for sales in my 3-Year Plan. The sales category would contain actual target revenue projections as well as the process that was developed for writing and closing contracts. Our business plan, particularly our 3-Year Plan, should include how we engage our potential clients, and how we follow up with our existing clients once they are interested in one of our products or strategies.

This list is really intended for a larger business, not an individual advisor. However, many of the items do apply to small business owners as well and should be taken into consideration. One of the items of particular interest to a financial advisor is risk and mitigation. What is the risk to an individual operation? Risk management is really at the heart of all life insurance and investment strategies. If a financial advisor has not implemented risk management strategies into their own practice, how can they convince a client of the need for these products? A good example is disability insurance. Protecting income sources is a fundamental risk management concept for most businesses, but it is particularly important for sole proprietors or incorporated professionals. For example, a dentist who runs a small practice may earn in the range of $500,000 corporately and perhaps $250,000 in salary and dividends. If a disability were to curtail their ability to run that practice, how could they ensure that it survives and can still provide income to maintain their lifestyle? A properly formulated disability policy in conjunction with business overhead coverage could be just the ticket. Our dentist could now safely learn to snowboard with the knowledge that a nasty accident would not bankrupt their business. An advisor should have similar coverage if they are running a solo office or a small agency.

The marketing and promotion category is of *extreme* importance in any 3-Year Plan since it will often represent a significant cost to our business – but it is a very necessary cost. Many businesses will have very high marketing costs in the beginning as they are trying to get the word out. Marketing budgets could climb as high as 25% of revenue in early spends on advertising, media spots, printing, news releases and other branding techniques. An established business may spend as little as 5% on marketing, particularly if they are not in a growth phase. They may want to attract only enough new business to replace client attrition. Either way, without a plan to attract potential clients and make them aware of our products, we will be floundering in our attempts to fill our sales funnel. And it is our sales funnel (sometimes called the sales pipeline) that is the lifeblood of our business. Sales cannot happen without prospects willing to listen to our story. And our story cannot be told unless we have a way to attract those prospects to our world. Marketing & Promotion strategies do just that – they attract prospects who are interested in our offerings.

Step one for our marketing plan is to establish a budget. If we do not allocate specific resources to our marketing initiatives, then we risk the possibility of either overspending and chewing into our working capital or underperforming by not funding a fully fleshed out marketing plan. In the 8-Step Dream Business Plan, we usually recommend a marketing budget of about 10% of annual revenue projection for a new advisor. As an example, if the advisor were projecting an annual gross revenue of $65,000 in their first year, we would expect they might have to spend $6,500.00 in marketing and promotional activities. What activities should they employ? Once again, that will vary depending on many factors:

- Age of the Advisor

- Natural Market/Target Market

- Size of Network

- Networking and Sales Acumen

- Budgetary Constraints

- Size of Current Book of Clients

- Amount of Working Capital

The amount of working capital is of paramount importance to a new independent advisor in our business. Remember, the new advisor has no revenue to start. Every dollar that is being spent on marketing, promotion, office space, transportation etc. is coming directly from either their savings or from business or personal loans. The nature of sales and revenue generation in the financial services sector is typically an extended sales cycle. If we are being diligent and responsible advisors, we must make sure that we do a proper job of understanding our client's situation and carefully assessing their needs and desires. We are not selling vacuums door to door (although that used to be the model for insurance sales many years ago). Today, properly trained financial advisors act as consultants rather than simply sales agents. What this means is that, in the independent channel of the industry, new advisors can expect to spend before they earn. That is why budgeting, projections and planning are necessary.

There is no "perfect" business plan. You just need one that will work for you and your idea. Some business plans are a few pages long, while others may be over 50 pages or more.

Do Inventory and Marshal Your Resources

As we begin to flesh out our 3-Year Plan, we need to start writing down an inventory of our current resources, including but not limited to: capital, contacts, partnerships, client and prospect lists, software and hardware. Obviously, we need to look carefully at our working capital since it may need to sustain us through the first months or even years of our business startup. Therefore, revenue projection is very important from day one. If we are going to begin as a solopreneur, we need to be realistic about the costs of doing business. Again, this is why our 5-Year Vision is also an important component to our 3-Year Plan. If we envision building an office with employees or new advisors, then we need to develop marketing plans that reflect our anticipated revenue needs. If, on the other hand, we are simply going to work out of a home office in the beginning and work from an extremely limited budget, then we might be able to create marketing plans at a reduced cost. This trade-off usually involves exchanging time for money. If we have enough working capital to run an extensive marketing campaign to drive prospects to our sales funnel, then we can expect to grow more quickly and potentially hire staff and attract other advisors in a short period of time. But if we find our resources limited, then we may have to resort to inexpensive marketing techniques such as cold calling, networking, building referral relationships and strategic alliances. And although capital is of paramount importance, it is important to identify all of our resources.

The Tax Man Cometh

In either case, we need to consider the tax ramifications of our business. There is nothing more ironic in our industry than a financial advisor who finds themselves in tax trouble. It's why we always recommend to our advisors that they find a competent accountant to assist them with setting up their business. The big question that most advisors usually ask about business structure is whether they should incorporate. Incorporation has several interesting benefits; however, it also comes with increased costs. As with most of our analyses, we need to look at the balance between the advantages of incorporation and the ongoing costs. For the solopreneur advisor who is just starting out, it typically does not pay to incorporate. Once they have achieved a certain level of revenue then incorporation may be a viable option. Accountant recommendations in this area vary with regard to the tipping point. Some contend that incorporation is a good idea as soon as it is economically viable (the figure $35,000 has been the lowest I have heard). Others say to wait until the business has grown to at least six figures and has sustainable cash flow. Whichever advice works for the new advisor, it makes sense to establish a relationship with an accountant – not just for their own purposes, but also as a resource to clients. It is important to build a network of professionals that can assist our business, and who can also assist your prospects and customers.

Brainstorm Strategic Alliances

Another very important reason to cultivate relationships with other professionals is to develop strategic alliances. A strategic alliance is a business relationship where the two parties share a similar market but do not compete directly with one another. In our industry, a good example would be a mortgage broker and a life insurance agent. Every mortgage that gets written offers the client life insurance as an optional benefit. There are forms of creditor insurance provided by lenders that the mortgage broker can use, but most experienced mortgage brokers understand that the creditor insurance may not be the best option for the client - so they will have a life insurance advisor to whom they will refer their clients. In turn, the life insurance agent will refer his clients to the mortgage broker or pay a referral fee to the broker for the client opportunity. Please note that not all provincial insurance regulators will allow for referral fees to be paid. National Best's head office resides in Alberta which does allow for referral fees under strict guidelines. This kind of strategic relationship is exactly what both professionals need to grow their business by extending their network.

That is all a strategic alliance really is – an extension of your network into someone else's network and vice versa. Can you think of other professionals that might make a good referral partner for a financial advisor? Here is a list to consider:

- Accountant

- Bookkeeper

- Tax Lawyer

- Wills & Estates Lawyer

- Mortgage Broker

- Business Evaluator

- Human Resource Professional

- Wealth Management Company

- Real Estate Professional

- Home & Auto Insurer

- Commercial Insurer

- Existing Clients

What do you think of this short list? Which of these professionals would make sense given your industry specialty or your target market? This is a list that can be brainstormed with your colleagues. Everyone might have a different ideal strategic partner depending on their target market.

Define your Market Clearly

Establishing a clearly defined market is important to our 3-Year Plan. In most businesses, trying to be all things to all people is a formula for failure. The more we can focus our energy on one or two key aspects of our industry, then the more detailed we can get when planning a marketing campaign.

Why?

Because we have narrowed down our market to a specific demographic, vertical, or customer profile. This process is known as segmentation. We look first at what our service provides and how we want to position ourselves in the marketplace. Then we try to zero in on the people or businesses who need that service the most, or who are underserved by our industry.

Perhaps we decide to focus on non-medical underwriting products for the hard to insure. When we look at the whole universe of possible clients, we would want to segment that vast number into different sub-categories so that we can see which segments might best fit the vision of our specialty. It might turn out that we are focused on cancer survivors. So, we become an expert at serving this market segment with life insurance solutions. We can now develop marketing plans specifically designed to inform this group of our unique value. But it also means that we can focus on new strategic partners – those service providers who also serve cancer sufferers and survivors. Now, a doctor can not only provide their patient with good news about remission, but also provide them with a professional who can help them get life insurance despite their previous illness. Now our advisor can direct their marketing resources to ads, brochures, mail outs, business cards and networking collateral that reflects this specific market segment. This, in turn, will make them memorable to most consumers and partners. If you are aware that I sell life insurance, you may think of me when you meet someone who is a potential client. But if you know me as the insurance guy who can get cancer survivors excellent life insurance coverage, then I am top-of-mind whenever you bump into my target market.

This kind of industry specialization and market segmentation produces significant results in the financial services world. In my early years in the industry, I tried to learn all the products and services in the life insurance universe. I saw it as a challenge to be well versed in all aspects of my industry. But as time went on, I found that my success depended on focusing on the products and strategies that most interested me – that I was passionate about. I was better off forming alliances with my colleagues who focused on products and services that were not my forte and let them handle the customers who had a need for their specialty. As an example, I do not have a fondness for Registered Education Savings Plans (RESPs). I much prefer if clients consider Participating Whole Life policies for their children as a savings and investment tool. However, if the client is keen on funding an RESP, then I will hand them over to my colleague, who is our resident RESP expert. Since Dave understands the product and providers better than I do, he serves the client at a higher quality level, and, in the end, everyone is better off. Collaboration has become a hallmark of National Best.

That is where our motto comes from: *Together We Are the Best*.

It simply means none of us has complete knowledge and information, but collectively we can cover all the bases. The same strategy applies in almost any small business. Find experts and let them serve your clients. Stick to your own area of competence and share your clients with other team members or other professionals who can create the very best customer experience available. That will keep you at the top of the customer service curve, which is our next area of interest.

Customer Service

Probably the most neglected area of business process in the financial services world, and particularly in the life insurance industry, is client service and follow-up. There are several historical reasons for this, but in recent years it relates more to the extremely high turnover and attrition rates in the industry.

Many new advisors don't make it through the first year in business. Some last a year or two and then find they cannot generate enough business to survive. Agencies are left with orphan clients who need to be serviced, but who don't provide enough value to induce the replacement advisor to make calls on them. It has been an industry issue for many years. The blame for this situation is shared, to some extent, between the insurance providers and the agencies. The reasons are too complex to delve into in this missive, but the industry is trying to address the issue via compliance regulations and forced changes to some of the agency models.

The 8 -Step Dream Business Plan tries to address this issue head-on. We want to make it clear to new advisors that they need to strategize and give serious consideration to financial services as a career, not just a money-making scheme bent on recruitment and cookie cutter product sales, but a true calling that requires careful thought and planning.

Those of us who have lived through various models in the industry understand that some models are not conducive to serving the client in a truly independent and ethical manner. The models are meant to serve the business goals of the agency and are not always in concert with the interests of individual advisors or clients. But even on the independent side of the industry, trying to be a full-service provider can be challenging. However, if a new advisor is to have any success, their business must be tackled with not only great élan, but with serious purpose and analytical planning. And when it comes to customer service, the earlier the planning the easier the journey.

44

Client Engagement – What is Your Sales Process?

Every business sells something. So, every business has a distribution system of some kind. In the world of financial services, sales are still considered to be a person-to-person activity. Even in the face of online applications, social media advertising and robo-advisors sprouting up everywhere, most agencies still look to recruit new advisors every day. One reason for the need for flesh and blood sales staff is that financial services is fundamentally a high trust business. No one really wants to trust their life savings to a cyber advisor who they will never meet or get to talk to one-on-one. However, with the new developments in compliance and the push to remove so-called hidden fees, robo-advice is becoming more popular all the time, particularly with younger generations. They are used to shopping online and have a high level of trust in internet transactions.

That being said, most people would still like a clear explanation of financial concepts from someone with the patience to sit down with them over a coffee and carefully outline all the nuances of insurance and investment products. This kind of client engagement represents the real value of an advisor. And providing clients and prospects with a quality experience when it comes to these interactions is key to the success of the relationship.

An important part of your 3-Year Plan is to develop a sales system. A sales system is composed of two parts:

1. Client Engagement

2. Selling Cycle

Client Engagement refers to the manner in which the advisor or the salesperson approaches, informs and onboards prospects, and follows up with existing clients.

The Selling Cycle refers to the mechanics and logistics of managing your pipeline or sales funnel.

The Selling Cycle can be likened to the *how* of the business and Client Engagement is the *why* of the business.

Our CRM (Customer Relationship Management) program can help us with both components of the Sales System. In the Selling Cycle, we will have prospects who want products immediately, some who want help in the near future and others for whom the products or strategies are on the back burner. We must be able to stay in touch with all of our prospects regardless of their urgency. Our CRM program is designed for this purpose. It will have a built-in calendar and task reminder that will alert us to any upcoming call or activity. Of course, the old adage of the data industry – GIGO (Garbage In, Garbage Out) – applies here big time. If you are going to implement a CRM program then it is incumbent upon you to make sure that you keep the information on your clients, prospects and partners up to date. Your business day should start by opening the CRM program and reviewing your calendar and task list. It should end by inputting the day's activities, notes, appointments and reminders, and a review of your next day's activity. Our sales funnel stays full and active when we are diligent at inputting our contacts, referrals and clients into the system and keeping up to date notes, emails and scheduled activities.

My CRM system has a great feature. It allows me to build processes for almost any kind of activity. As an example, if I have just delivered a new policy to a client, I can set up a series of reminders for follow-up activity. For instance, I will be reminded a week after the delivery to send a thank you note. Two weeks later, I will send an email asking if the client has any questions about the policy. Three weeks later, I might send a short survey asking for feedback with regard to their customer experience with my process. Four weeks later, I will be reminded to send a gift coffee card asking for referrals... etc. All of these activities can be pre-programmed for any business event and can be implemented with just one click of a button.

Client Engagement, on the other hand, refers to the way we treat our clients and prospects. At National Best, for example, one of our founders, Dr. Maria Lizak, developed a process that we still use today. It looks like this:

The smiley face may strike you as being a bit juvenile. But when broken down, you will see that it is a perfect client engagement system for not only our industry, but for any company that is in the relationship business. It is even the perfect way to build contacts via business networking.

Appreciate – Look for things that are positive about your client or prospect and congratulate them for their situation even if they are struggling.

Connect - Try to find common ground with your client and ways in which you are like them and can understand their position.

Discover – Ask questions to uncover what is most important to the client right now, today.

Share – Only share information or strategies with your client once you understand their most important issues, and make the information relevant to their needs.

47

Confirm – Review carefully to make sure that your shared information and transaction does fulfill your client's needs.

Follow-Up – Return to the client at a later date to make sure they are still served properly by your product or service.

Appreciate – Thank your client for their trust and set up a scheduled follow-up program and appreciation marketing campaign.

Follow-Up and the CRM Program

The key to both sales and customer service is a systematized follow-up process. Almost any business coach will preach the need for ongoing engagement with clients and prospects. There are all kinds of business rules and theories about the number of times a prospect must hear about your product or service (the current industry jargon refers to "touches"). Some say that it takes between five and seven, meaning emails, ads, phone calls, thank you notes, newsletters etc. Other numbers that are bandied about are 12 touches, 15 touches, I have even heard 25 touches for some industries. Whatever number you find works for your target market is the number you should use. And the only way to discover that number is to have a follow-up system that allows you to track your "touches" and report on your success. And in my experience, the only way to achieve that measurable goal is to have a robust CRM program.

A CRM program is a software that allows you to create a database of information about your clients, prospects and business partners. Without one, it will be almost impossible to keep track of all your calls, emails, notes, contact information, product info per client, commissions and, most importantly, follow-up activities. A good CRM program will provide information at your fingertips. We can sort information in a relational way so that we can target certain clients or prospects with email info, product updates, upcoming events or any other "touch" that will keep our business top of mind. It will also remind us about annual reviews and seasonal activities, and it is a repository for all of our client's business with us.

In my previous career in transportation, I got used to using a CRM program to track my sales activities and that is where I first found the value of a true relational database. However, when I moved to the financial services industry, I did not begin with a CRM program. As mentioned, start up for an independent advisor is an extended sales process most times, and there is no real need to collect data when you are working with only a few dozen files. The paper-based system was fine for the first year. But very soon, it became clear to me that a digital system was going to be necessary to keep up with all the information and follow-up. By the time you reach 100 clients, the only way to stay on top of client service, sales pipeline management and compliance (and not have anything fall through the cracks) was to have a solid CRM program. My recommendation is to purchase a good CRM program as soon as possible. Even if your agency has a client database it does not mean that it is a robust, programmable, relational program that can provide the kind of information you will need.

Lack of follow-up is a business killer. Too many opportunities and potential prospects get left behind if an advisor does not have a system. Many agencies will provide their advisors with some form of CRM system, but I have rarely seen one that is robust enough to encompass all the aspects of our industry. That is the reason for making sure that your CRM is fully relational and programmable. The CRM provides the backbone of the follow-up system. It has to take into account all of the data and the communication that will support your target market.

As an example, if you are an independent life agent and you use a number of different providers to serve your clients (as any independent should), then you will want to direct specific information to certain clients or prospects, based on their segmentation in your system. Foresters Financial is one of Canada's leading life companies when it comes to serving the family market. As the only fraternal in Canada, they use their profit to provide benefits and services back to their members (policy holders) and their communities. This could involve volunteer charity events, family outings, or other member benefits. Your CRM program will allow you to direct specific information to your clients who hold Foresters policies, keeping them updated on upcoming events, changes to their policies or new Foresters offerings. In the same way, you might want to provide a monthly market update to all of your investment clients, particularly if they have funds in a market that is undergoing high volatility. Too many clients feel forgotten. With regular newsletters, targeted updates and scheduled reviews and meetings, the CRM keeps you in touch with your clients and assures them that you still care about your relationship.

The CRM is most useful and most powerful for the sales pipeline process. Most good CRM products will allow you to build in scheduled process reminders, meetings and emails. The key to not letting a prospect slip through the cracks is to stay in touch and stay relevant. No one likes spam so your CRM should not be a spam generating device sending out reminders about your upcoming seminar every day for weeks on end. It should be set up to target your market segments with information that is a value to the prospect or client at the time they need it. This is no easy task, but a strong CRM system will help you carry out this important follow-up process.

I have seen some old school advisors who still use a rolodex and recipe cards in boxes along with client files to provide good service. It can be done. But in today's technological whirlwind, a well set up CRM program is a must for the modern advisor.

Compliance

Our 3-Year Plan is not complete until we address another important issue. Almost any independent business startup needs to review the relevance and management of compliance. Even franchise operations have internal rules that must be adhered to. Today, almost every service business has some form of government or internal regulatory control. It is vitally important to any new business that they understand the regulatory regime that governs their business activities and to ensure that their employees are well-versed in these rules. This is particularly true in the financial services industry, which is highly regulated, and for good reason – we deal with people's money and financial well-being. In financial services, the rules surrounding compliance deal mostly with ethical behavior and transparency. In other industries, you might add safety as a primary regulatory concern. In any case, everyone in the organization should be kept up to speed with the rules and any ongoing changes that occur. More and more industries are realizing that the position of compliance/safety officer holds a vital role in the organization.

In financial services, every agency will have a compliance officer. Compliance seminars and workshops are generally considered to be mandatory attendance in most agencies. From a sales perspective, compliance can often seem like a barrier to writing contracts. Independent advisors are particularly susceptible to this mindset since their business is commission based and any outside forces that detract from an efficient sales process can appear to be a detriment to their business. However, in general, we can consider this to be a wrong way of thinking. Trying to skirt the regulatory regime and bend the rules in order to produce short-term gains loses sight of the long-term goal of compliance as it relates to the individual advisor. Once again, for advisors who are playing a long game, losing some sales due to compliance processes and the burden of additional paperwork is a small price to pay for a set of clean client files that will pass audit without any fines or penalties. And agencies that fail to implement a mandatory and detailed compliance program are setting themselves up for failure.

The financial services industry in Canada has gone through some significant changes over the last few years that relate to fees and transparency, particularly in the investment sector. There has been a backlash against embedded fees in the investment sector and we see this reflected in regulatory changes, transparency rules and business models. There are good arguments for and against the kinds of fees that are charged, or have been charged, in the Canadian marketplace. It is very important in any transaction that clients are aware of any associated fees, and that they are pointed out and explained. At National Best we made it a rule that all advisors had to explain exactly how they were paid, the cost to the client and any other fees inherent in the transaction. Many clients are not so concerned about the fees themselves (they understand that we need to get paid) they just want to know and understand why they are being charged.

One of the ways that agencies and independent advisors can ensure a strong adherence to regulatory mandates is to develop a culture of compliance within their business plan. At National Best, our 3-Year Plan involves regular compliance training as well as internal audits to ensure compliance. But more than that, creating a compliant culture involves setting up a code of ethics and outlining the fundamental values of the organization.

National Best uses the acronym CRISP to outline its core values, which are essential to any successful business or advisor:

Commitment – We keep our word

Respect– We value and care about people

Integrity – We endeavor to do the right thing every time

Sharing – We freely exchange knowledge and ideas, working in harmony with cooperation, collaboration, and camaraderie

Professional Excellence– We give our best, providing exceptional service for all

As a company or advisor's business grows, it becomes more and more important to explicitly define the core values that drive the culture, the brand and the business strategies. It is essential to cultivate respect, integrity, and professional excellence, whether working as a solopreneur or working with other advisors to share ideas, knowledge and expertise.

At National Best we created a unique culture of mentorship that fosters a willingness to share training, talents, skills, and knowledge with our teammates which, in turn, provides the highest level of expertise and mentorship for our clients. Even our totally independent advisors see the value of the sharing of ideas and skill sets. As mentioned before, having a specialty and leaning on other advisors to service clients has become a hallmark of the National Best experience for new advisors and clients.

Although the financial services industry has evolved over the years, and although it still may be perceived as a traditional sales process, most agencies train advisors using consultative sales techniques rather than the old persuasion tricks that were common in the industry decades ago. Being a consultant puts the client first and the sale second.

In addition to core values, a code of ethics is also a valuable tool to remind advisors that they have a set of standards to live up to when it comes to client service. I have belonged to a BNI (Business Networking International) chapter for over 7 years and they have a very strong code of ethics that allows new members to clearly understand their responsibilities within the organization.

Here is the code of ethics at National Best:

To ensure that high standards are maintained, we have defined the standards to which we expect National Best advisors to adhere. *

Our Commitment

National Best is committed to ensuring that the sales process is of the highest integrity and focused on client needs. These measures have been put in place to ensure that clients are completely satisfied with the product they purchase. Our advisors commit to the following:

1. Compliance with the Code, Laws, Rules, Regulations and Company Policies & Procedures: Maintaining compliance with all federal and provincial laws and regulations and following internal standards governing the sales process.

2. Avoiding Conflict of Interest: Conducting their business affairs in a manner that ensures that their private or personal interests do not

conflict with the interests of clients, including conflicts that result in personal, financial or other gain.

3. Acting Competently, Professionally and with Integrity: Dealing fairly with their clients and National Best. Providing services, advice or information only where they are licensed and competent to do so.

4. Needs Selling and Continuous Service: Identifying the needs of the client before offering advice and providing continuous attention to these needs.

5. Disclosure: Providing full and accurate disclosure of all facts required to allow the client to make an informed decision.

6. Priority of Client's Interests: Giving priority at all times to the interests of the client when providing advice or when deferring to the advice of others who are licensed and specialized in that area of client need.

7. Confidentiality: Holding the personal and business information of clients in the strictest of confidence and complying with personal privacy acts and regulations.

8. Documentation: Providing clients with written or electronic copies of any advice given and retaining sufficient information in a client file to demonstrate the appropriateness of a sale.

Advisors representing National Best or its affiliates must adhere to the Code of Ethics. Please refer to the National Best Advisor Resources Website for full details of our Code of Ethics.

Education

Finally, in our 3-Year Plan we must figure out who we want to be. As with almost any profession, we need training. And in many independent businesses, we need ongoing education in order to maintain our professional designations. This is true for dentists, electricians, lawyers, accountants, and financial advisors. In a way, it is true of almost any job. Even the most basic kinds of employment go through changes that require upgrading in knowledge, whether it involves new technologies, new techniques or just new ideas. Human beings, generally, are in a constant state of learning. It is our nature.

It is important to relate your professional training to your target market. If you want to help families manage their money, there are licenses and training that relate to that market. For instance, MFDA (Mutual Funds), IIROC (Stock Broker), Exempt Market (Private Equity Investments), CFP (Chartered Financial Planner), LLQP (Life Insurance Advisor), etc. This list in our industry is quite extensive depending on who you want to serve, in what manner you would like to serve, and what products, concepts and strategies you consider valuable to your client.

In other areas of our industry, you may want to directly manage larger portfolios, pension plans or hedge funds. In that case, other designations are necessary — CFA (Chartered Financial Analyst) or CIM (Chartered Investment Manager). Regardless of your target market, lifelong learning is a part of every business and so it should be incorporated into your own plan.

I personally hold my life license and an exempt market license to service my clients. I am a big believer in protection products for families and business owners. So, my interests are skewed to the Life Insurance industry and their vast list of products:

- ✓ Life Insurance

- ✓ Critical Illness Insurance

- ✓ Disability Insurance

- ✓ Long Term Care Insurance

- ✓ Travel insurance

- ✓ Business Overhead Insurance

- ✓ Segregated Funds (the Life industry's Mutual Funds)

- ✓ Annuities

- ✓ Health and Dental Plans

- ✓ Health Spending Accounts

- ✓ Group Benefits

Even within these product categories there are many options and variations that are built to fit almost any client situation. As an example, life insurance comes in three flavors in Canada: Term, Whole and Universal, but even within these categories there are many variations and specialty products that work to serve Canadians. One advantage of being a true broker in the business is that we get exposed to all the providers and the products they consider their sweet spots. However, staying on top of that knowledge pool is an ongoing and difficult task. It is another reason why we encourage specialization. If we have colleagues who know a certain product inside and out, we don't have to understand every detail, we just need to know that the product or strategy exists and leverage their talent for the benefit of the client. This is why ongoing education has to be a key component of our 3-Year Plan.

Finally, education does not just mean securing and maintaining a professional designation or trade. It also means self-development. If it's our plan to serve our clients to the very best of our ability, then we need more than just some book training and a title. We need to develop other skill sets and life experience so that we can provide a customer experience that sets us apart – that creates a truly unique value proposition for the client. Education can help us achieve this part of our plan.

Education for all humans is a daily event. The very nature of our existence sets forth new information, lessons, and experiences that change and mold our character and our understanding. In our chapter "The 1-Day Task List", we will see how to recognize and incorporate education and learning into our daily routine.

Conclusion

As you might have guessed, our chapter on planning is by far the longest and most far-reaching section. That is because planning is the key to confident action. Without action, we just have our Dream and our Vision to admire. That admiration does not serve us, nor any of our friends, colleagues or clients. We must lay out a road map, plot our course, turn on the engine and drive. That is the essence of the 3-Year Plan and the ultimate goal of the 8-Step Dream Business Plan.

As mentioned, the 3-Year Plan is not a static document. It is a living document that needs to be revisited regularly. It needs to be tested, measured, tweaked and implemented. There are various ways in which you can house your 3-Year Plan.

Some examples include:

1. Notebook (Paper and Pen)

2. Word Doc (or another digital manual)

3. Excel Spread Sheet (especially for the numbers)

4. Project Software (especially shared software if you have a team)

Or, you might use a combination of these to help with your planning. Regardless, once our 3-Year Plan is in place, we need to work on the details of our first year in business and every year thereafter. Next, we develop our 1-Year Goal.

Immediate Action Steps:

- Book a time in your calendar in the next month to write down your plan for your business. Ensure you will have at least an hour of uninterrupted time. This may be scheduled a week or two after your vision and mission exercise as part of the regular business-planning sessions that you have scheduled. You will want to ensure that you have your dream board and your vision and mission statements with you to inspire you. *Do it now.*

- Text or email a trusted friend or colleague about your intention to spend this time creating your business plan. *Do it now.*

- Download the business planning worksheet and save it to your device. Have a quick look at the questions (also listed in the chapter above) and write down any answers that come to mind. This will help you get started with a business planning session. *Do it now.* https://mailchi.mp/93c0d198a165/8-step-dream-business-plan-worksheet

Here are a few additional resources that can help you to get your business plan up and running:

- *The Canada Business Network*: this collaborative arrangement among federal departments and agencies, provincial and territorial governments, and not-for-profit entities has valuable information on why you need a business plan, how to write a business plan, and business planning frequently asked questions.
- *The Business Development Bank of Canada:* this financial institution owned by the Government of Canada has a free business plan template and an article on the basics of writing a business plan.
- *Our team of in-house experts:* we can help you research, plan, and review your business plan. Contact us today!

Step 4. The 1-Year Goal

"A goal properly set is halfway reached."

– Zig Ziglar

We now have a 10-Year Dream that we are passionate about, a 5-Year Vision that describes how we want our business to look, the mission to serve our clients that will get us there, and a 3-Year Plan that addresses our medium-term business structure and processes including: marketing, sales, compliance, strategic partners, education and exit strategy.

Now it is time to put all those big ideas to work. This is where the rubber meets the road. It is time to build our 1-Year Goal and face the numbers head-on. The primary purpose of our 1-Year Goal is to set revenue numbers. Every profitable business aims to create enough operating income to pay all their expenses and have a healthy profit at the end of their fiscal year. The same is true whether you are a solopreneur, a partnership, an agency or a large corporation. In the case of an independent financial advisor, profit equals lifestyle. In other words, their profit represents their household budget. So, when it comes to breaking down the numbers for the 1- Year Goal, our first task on an individual basis is to complete a cash flow analysis. It is helpful to provide a cash flow sheet to your clients and recommend that they track their spending for three months. When projected over the remaining nine months it becomes a very accurate picture of expenses and spending. Most of us could get close to the annual numbers simply by adding up our monthly expenses, but the more data we can collect, the more accurate our final numbers.

Once we have accounted for all of our household expenses, we can add these to our business expenses and come up with a total which we can use as our annual goal. That was easy! But we have forgotten something.

We also need to remember our medium-term plan and our long-term vision and dream. These items also have numbers attached to them and, typically, they are numbers that will grow year by year. In order to make sure we include these numbers in our 1-Year Goal, or at least keep them visible so we can keep our eye on our island paradise on the horizon, we should consider three sets of numbers instead of one.

But before we look at structuring those revenue goals, let's take a quick look at the current wisdom surrounding how to set a workable goal. Virtually every sales or business coach who discusses goals with their client will talk about SMART goals:

- *Specific*

- *Measurable*

- *Assignable or Attainable*

- *Realistic*

- *Timely*

There is some debate over the origin of the term 'SMART Goals' - but many sources cite a paper written in November of 1981 in Spokane, Washington by George T. Doran, a consultant and former Director of corporate planning for Washington Water and Power Company. He published a paper titled *"There's a S.M.A.R.T. way to Right Management's Goals and Objectives."*

Others claim that it was a collaborative effort of the management team with whom George Doran was working. Whatever the case may be, smart goals have become a standard of business planning. Over the years, some of the words in the acronym have changed. For instance, the original term for the letter "A" was Assignable, however, over the years it has changed to Attainable and sometimes Achievable. Personally, I prefer Assignable. In my mind, a realistic goal would, by definition, be attainable or achievable. Also, assignable makes much more sense in a team environment in which a number of different individuals may be contributing to achieve the result.

The SMART goal concept can be used in almost any context. However, in the 8-Step Dream Business Plan, we are going to use it to set our annual revenue numbers which represents the key component of our One-Year goal.

Specific

The current thinking is that the more specific the goal the greater the chance that it can be accomplished. Not everyone agrees with this statement, however. In some cases, business consultants will argue that more generalized goals will still induce action, which is the object of goal setting, but will not produce disappointment when the specific goal is not attained. There is some validity to this argument but for our purposes we are going to stick to specific numbers, since that is what we are dealing with in terms of revenue. After all, no one wants to make some money, or a bunch of money or a whole lot of money – *they want to make $100,000.*

For a new advisor, we have recommended working out a budget that will produce a necessary revenue number in order to build the business and pay household expenses. This would be a minimum goal. In Canada, various sources site the average salary of financial advisors at approximately $60,000 per year for a full-time position. This might be a good starting point for our new advisors. An experienced advisor might have a larger number in mind. Whatever the number is, it should be specific so that we can reverse engineer the total and break it down into smaller units to fit our marketing and sales process. Now we can fit it into our 3-Month Review, our 1-Month Schedule, our 1-Week Target and, ultimately, our 1-Day Task List.

Measurable

A SMART goal is one that we can measure. In our 1-Year Goal this may seem quite simple if all we are doing is calculating revenue. We see the numbers with every pay cheque or commission deposit. But simply adding up the numbers every week or two does not really fulfill the planning around our 1-Year Goal. We need to have feedback once we input the data to tell us how we are doing. At National Best, we have a spreadsheet that does exactly that. It has been developed to automatically add up the numbers, then compare them to our stated goals and provide us with a variance – either positive or negative. The value of this kind of measuring is in the behavioral cycle that it can create. Most people will pick up their game if they see that they are falling behind the target. The measurement can give us motivation to do a little extra to make sure we hit our targets the next week, month or quarter. But what if we overachieve and exceed our goals for the month? Common wisdom tells us that most people will ease off on the pedal and take a break. If we are in a business growth stage, this is not recommended practice. Later in the chapter, we will show you how to avoid the production success trap.

Assignable or Attainable

Both of these terms have been used to define SMART goals over the years. The first reason is that no one ever achieves a goal all alone. Take one of the most individual sports – golf. The best golfers in the world hire a cadre of coaches, caddies and sports psychologists to support their game. Independent financial advisors and other solopreneurs are much like golf pros. We think we are doing business all by ourselves when, in fact, we are supported by supplier wholesalers, inside support staff, accountants, colleagues and strategic partners. If we are building a brokerage, then we can add new recruits, employees and partners to the mix. What this means is that we can reach our goals by assigning tasks, or even production, to others. This allows us to amplify our results via team building. As in our 3-Year Plan, we need to know who we want on the team and how they will contribute. In turn, we may be assigned certain jobs or responsibilities to assist others in achieving their goals – echoing the famous Zig Ziglar quote: *"You will get all you want in life, if you help enough other people get what they want."* In fact, that is the goal of any entrepreneur – to provide people with a quality product or service that they need and want.

The other reason to choose Assignable over Attainable is our next word in the acronym – Realistic. By definition, a Realistic goal would have to be Attainable. If it were not, then where do we find the rationale for our numbers? It makes no sense for a new advisor to set a target of $2M revenue in the first year unless they have a natural market that would justify that goal. I am not a law of attraction fan in this area of planning. Just thinking about something or believing that it could be will not make it so. The only things that get us to our goal are passion, purpose, planning and implementation. And the more of that plan that we can assign to others, the more likely we will reach our target.

Realistic

There is a famous Will Smith viral video where he rants about how being realistic is no way to achieve greatness. He has a point, but I think what he really means is being mediocre will not breed success. When we define a goal as being realistic, all we mean is that, given the right circumstances, we should be able to work to achieve it. Mr. Smith is trying to tell us that if we don't aim high enough (be unrealistic) then we will be unchallenged by our goal and take the easy path to false success. I have a lot of sympathy for this point of view since I am the kind of person who likes to reward myself for daily, weekly, monthly or quarterly achievements. I think that a feedback of congratulations helps me stay motivated to go after the next project or goal that I have set. But sometimes I find myself relaxing after having achieved a particular goal. I think this is just human nature. In fact, most current business coaching gurus recommend regular breaks from our working schedule. It seems that we work too hard and for too long in North America. Personally, I don't feel I work hard enough most of the time. However, in order to set and achieve a realistic goal we should be breaking down the number of hours it will take to accomplish our marketing, sales and other measurable activities. As long as the hours of work match our sales close ratios, it should be a realistic goal.

But what if my estimation of a realistic goal was not accurate? If we don't have past data to work with then how can we know what is realistic and what is not? As mentioned, if we are a new advisor or are new to business, we can lean on our colleagues or even our competitors to find out what information is available to help us with our sale's close ratios. But this still will not help us if we are in a growth phase of our business. And in financial services, until you have achieved a book of business that satisfies your greatest income desire, then you are essentially always in growth mode. Even when you have built a sufficient book of business you must still stay diligent in the marketing and sales department in order to take care of normal attrition. So, a realistic goal today may not be a realistic goal tomorrow. And, if I do hit my goal quicker than I had anticipated, how do I reestablish a higher goal that makes sense?

As I mentioned, in my case, were I to hit a goal ahead of schedule, I would take a break. And although that may be a good time to go on a vacation, it may also be the best time to crank up my business and use the momentum of my current success to propel me forward to a higher goal. Later in this chapter we will show you how to solve this issue using a multi-goal approach.

Timely

A SMART goal must be timely – in other words, it must have an end date. That is why we use it for our 1-Year Goal. Not only are we going to define the exact amount of revenue we are working toward, but we are defining how long it will take us to achieve it. The 1-year Goal allows us to break down and analyze the numbers so that we can plan our 1-Month Schedule and our 1-Week Targets. However, there is no reason that we cannot use the same SMART goal method for shorter-term, or longer-term goals. It is simply a matter of changing the drop-dead date. We might have a project that we want to accomplish in three months or six weeks, or even five years (our 5-Year Vision). If we can apply the SMART goal concept to it, then it will help us stay on track and measure our progress. Writing this book was a SMART goal. I broke down the process into a variety of SMART components and set an end date. I found that writing first thing in the morning after my workout was the best time to get things done, and, since I worked out Monday, Wednesday and Friday, those were my writing days. Further, I calculated the number of chapters over the period that I chose and estimated the number of words I would have to write on average to finish on time. Of course, nothing goes exactly as planned so some days were made up on weekend mornings or late evenings. But once I have the structure defined, I could enter it into my calendar as a regular recurring activity. That helps to anchor the activity and make sure that it does not get skipped.

Minimum – Target - Outrageous

Now that we have a 10-Year Dream of success, a 5-Year Vision of how our business should look, a 3-Year Plan to implement to achieve our dreams and visions, and a 1-Year Goal to help keep us on track and define our activity, we need to ask an important question:

What happens if we achieve our 1-Year Goal early?

This may seem like a strange question, but for many people completing the goal means that they can take a break and relax. There is certainly merit in rewarding oneself for a job well done. And a break or a vacation may be exactly the right thing to do after achieving an important goal. But when it comes to our 1-Year goal, vacation or not, we want to continue our momentum. Of course, we could sit down and simply rework our goals - increase them or set up a new mini goal for the rest of the year. However, I believe in using a different strategy for the 8-Step Dream Business Plan - a more optimistic approach. Instead of just setting one goal for the year, I set three goals:

1. Minimum

2. Target

3. Outrageous

We adopted this approach at National Best from the work of Raymond Aaron who is a well-known business and life coach. Mr. Aaron defines the terms this way:

Minimum

Minimum is defined as what you would normally achieve based on your past record. It is not based on any kind of hope or arbitrary large target, but rather on the reality of what you have achieved previously. Obviously, if you have no past history, then some arbitrary number has to be used and in the case of the 8-Step Dream Business Plan, we define minimum as the amount of income you need to pay for your lifestyle. Of course, everyone has a different definition of lifestyle so what we really mean is: what is the minimum income required to pay for your personal budget? This number can vary widely depending on circumstances. For instance, a new advisor who is young, single and still living at home in their parents' basement may require a smaller minimum than an advisor with a family and a mortgage. Whatever the minimum goal is, it should allow the advisor to sustain their business. This is much the same for any small businessperson. Their business model should be set up so that, in the normal course of marketing and sales, they are least able to survive and build their business.

Target

Raymond Aaron's definition of a target goal is a number that is slightly beyond our reach. It must be a number big enough to force us to carefully evaluate our business plan. If we are sure that we can achieve our minimum goal, our target goal is meant to get us thinking about the next level of activity and planning required to build our company or our practice. Our minimum goal is meant to be easy to reach so that we can feel good about achieving success. But our target goal is meant not only to make us feel good, but to feel much more confident in our abilities and in our plan. By hitting our target goal, we know that we have done a better-than-average job, not only for ourselves but for our clients and our company. And, let's face it, no one wants to be average or have a mediocre business. Thus, the need for a target goal that will keep us focused and reaching higher. But remember, it must not be too far out of reach. It should be like a jar on the top shelf that we can almost reach on our tiptoes but instead requires us to be a bit more creative and find ourselves a stepstool.

Outrageous

Mr. Aaron defines the outrageous goal as that which you know you cannot achieve. I believe he means that it should be more of a dream than what anyone would consider a realistic number. The 8-Step Dream Business Plan takes a different approach. We know that there are business models and advisors in our industry who make an exceedingly large income. Of course, like all industries, the ultra-high earners are a minority. But because they exist, we know that those income numbers are achievable. Now, will these business models or high incomes be accessible to everyone in the industry? Probably not, given the limited and specific markets that they serve. However, there is a wide range of markets and business models that can produce extraordinary results. At National Best, we ask our advisors to imagine one of those models and markets working in their 8-Step Dream Business Plan. As an example, a new advisor may have started out serving the family market and is comfortable producing an annual income of $50,000. That would be their minimum. Their target goal might be $75,000 based on acquiring one new client per month. That is a very reasonable stretch for someone who is already reasonably successful. However, the outrageous goal might be $150,000 based on marketing additional products to their current clients and targeting one referral per client over the next year. It may seem impossible to sell an additional product to every single client and to get every client to provide a qualified referral; however, once this program is implemented it will inevitably produce results.

Perhaps the new result helps us achieve our target goal. This means that next year our 8-Step Dream Business Plan will have a 1-Year Goal where the target has now become the minimum and our target goal is edging closer to that which used to be outrageous. This process can be used at any step in our business model. Many advisors find that as their practice matures, they move from servicing families to servicing businesses. They might move from providing life insurance and critical illness policies to marketing group benefit plans and group investment plans. This evolution is facilitated by always having an outrageous goal that requires a reworking of our business in order to achieve the result.

Client Engagement System

As I mentioned in the previous chapter, the sales process, or the way in which we deal with clients in order to provide our products and solutions, is fundamental to our business. Some might argue that this topic really belongs in the 3-Year Plan. However, I prefer to think of it as a part of our 1-Year Goal because it is part of our everyday culture. Although it is not a number, I believe that the way we deal with our clients can be measured using qualitative techniques, and that including it in our 1- Year Goal helps to remind us that our client engagement system is inextricably linked to our production success. Once again, here is the National Best client engagement system as developed by Dr. Maria Lizak:

I like to think of this as the friendliest sales strategy in the financial services industry. It represents a truly consultative model of engagement with clients and is far from the old sales model of getting the client to sign on the dotted line no matter what.

Let's go over the words in detail.

Appreciate

Before we speak to our clients about products. Before we outline features and benefits. Before we speak to our clients about strategies and planning. Even before we ask them to provide us with a financial snapshot so that we can be sure that our recommendations are sound. Before all that – we are trained to appreciate our clients for who they are and what they do. It is our belief that before you can serve anyone, regardless of your industry or profession, you must have more than a superficial understanding of your client's situation. It is vitally important to have an empathetic understanding of your client. Try to put yourself in their shoes and see the world through their eyes. If your job is to serve them to the best of your ability, then you must try to understand how they feel about their history, their current circumstances and their future. This may seem like an impossible task, particularly during an initial consultation. After all, we are just getting to know each other, and most new clients have a natural trepidation about revealing too much information to someone new. And that's okay. Our job isn't to try and delve into their personal and business lives to the extent that we are acting like psychologists. What we want to do is observe carefully.

If we are meeting in the client's home or business, we can scan the room to pick up on clues about their interests, their background, their family and their personal tastes. It doesn't take Sherlock Holmes to understand that your client is an avid deep-sea fisherman if there is a massive stuffed marlin on the wall above his desk. Also, we need to be on the lookout for body language and their reaction to certain questions or topics. Also, take note of how they dress and how they comport themselves during the meeting. Are they dressed formally? Do they act in a strictly businesslike manner? Or are they dressed casually and are they interested in a bit of chitchat before getting down to the business at hand? Trying to gain a deeper understanding of our client by careful observation is a part of appreciation. This helps us to break down the client/salesman dynamic that is the standard for many initial business meetings. We want to know our new client as a human being first and as a potential customer second. By showing interest in what interests them from the very beginning we set ourselves up as consultants rather than order takers. The deeper our appreciation of this new relationship, the more accurately we will be able to gain insight into their true needs and desires. In order to make financial recommendations, we need to learn about their dreams so that we can empower them to succeed. Appreciation for others and their dreams naturally leads us to develop connections with them.

Connect

Finding a connection with a new person is not that hard. The concept of five degrees of separation holds true in almost all situations. By asking a few simple questions, we can usually find common ground with almost anyone who lives in the same city as we do. Even people who live in different cities have a common experience. All we have to do is tap into that experience to make a connection. However, the deeper the connection, the more significant the relationship. And we can find those deeper connections via our appreciation. When I visit a new client and I notice a guitar sitting in a corner I always ask them who plays? The reason I do this is because in a previous life I was a professional musician. Often, I find out that the client plays regularly, not simply as a hobby, but with a weekend dance band. This can lead to a full out conversation on musicianship, band dynamics, the nature of playing live and other music related experiences. That common musical experience can create an instant and deep connection. The deeper the connection, the easier the communication. It is much easier to chat with someone who you know has shared your experiences than with someone you know nothing about.

Not every client encounter is going to produce such a shared experience. As mentioned, some clients are very reticent to open up about their personal life or even about their current financial situation. In that case, finding a deep connection can be much more difficult. But there is always a connection. Even the most superficial connection can create an initial level of trust. It is simply a matter of finding a topic, an experience or an event that you have in common. Every Canadian who is standing in a line up at the bank will comment on the weather because, if nothing else, we all have that experience in common every single day. Once you have made a connection, it is time for discovery.

The first two steps of our client engagement involve conversation, asking questions and trying to learn more about our clients so that we can discern their true concerns and intentions. This leads naturally to our third step: discovering the issues that are most important to them. The only way to truly discover their most pressing need is to listen carefully. The listening part of this equation cannot be stressed enough. And we must be actively listening. Active listening involves not simply hearing the words that are said but trying to understand the meaning behind the words themselves. In an initial meeting, most clients do their best not to reveal too much about their personal and financial life. They need to feel comfortable with this new person who has arrived to ask them very intimate questions that they may not even discuss with their spouse or their children. But if we listen carefully to their words, and even more importantly observe their body language, we can often tell exactly which words are causing stress. From there, we can direct the conversation to learn more about those stressors. There are many books on understanding body language and lots of information on the Internet, and I fully recommend reviewing this material. If we are to truly help our clients, then we must know what is most important to them.

I am adamant about entering into a new client relationship without a specific sales agenda, particularly at the discovery stage. As professionals, it may be that we can see some important financial matters that should be dealt with, such as sufficient life insurance and disability coverage. But if our client tells us that their greatest concern is their credit card debt, then our job as professional advisors is to address that issue first. This approach may cause some debate, and we certainly don't want to leave any gaps in a customer's financial plan. However, customers will be much more willing to consider other products and strategies that we consider to be important if, in the beginning, we address that which is most important to them. For many years, I believed that if I were simply to show a prospect the numbers and provide them with a rational, logical argument for a particular product or strategy, then I would have done my job properly and provided them with understanding and viable options.

What I learned is that most people may say they care about the numbers and understanding the strategies, but all of that is typically secondary. What we really want to discover is what our clients truly care about. That means - what relationships in their life have the most meaning to them and what is it that they love? Tapping into their deepest emotions provides much more significant information about what they really need than simply recording information and data. So, in our discovery step we should always be on the lookout for the deeper meaning in our conversation.

Share

We are only allowed to share our expertise and our professional opinion with our client after we have appreciated their situation, made a connection with them to build trust and rapport and discovered the most burning issue in their current financial situation. To enter into a client relationship with a preconceived strategy or product is wrong. Some of the business models in our industry train their advisors in these kinds of cookie-cutter solutions in order to increase production and maximize commissions. There is no place in our industry for this kind of client engagement process. If the life insurance industry in Canada wants to be taken seriously as true financial consultants, then we have to quit selling life insurance like a commodity.

Every advisor should be trained to fully understand and be able to explain all the products they sell in detail so that every single client is aware of what's available to them. Through proper discovery they will always be led to the correct product, and it is not our job to use antiquated sales techniques to convince them to purchase one particular product or another. Our job is to educate. We share knowledge. Often, my colleagues in the industry have scoffed at my approach when it comes to client education. Their claim is that most clients don't want the education they just want to be told what to do. I agree there are some clients who aren't that interested in understanding the minute details of a product or strategy; however, I would much rather lose a sale due to over education than gain a client who is not fully aware of what they were purchasing.

Too many times in our industry I have encountered clients who were sold a universal life policy as a retirement plan only to discover years later that the illustration was exaggerated in terms of return and that it was clearly underfunded from the beginning. Usually, when I question these clients and ask them if they were shown any alternatives to the strategy, the answer is no. They were never shown other options such as term insurance or whole life insurance. This is a travesty. We must share our knowledge equally with all clients in order to provide the utmost level of service. This is what true client engagement is all about.

Not only do we share our knowledge and our skills, we also share our network. This means that if the client requires services in other areas of their life, we should recommend qualified and vetted professionals to assist them. At National Best, for example, our culture of collaboration means that we will always turn to our colleagues, either internally or externally, to provide complete financial planning for our clients - even if it means deferring our own sale in order to accommodate the most urgent elements of planning. A good example of this is in will and estate documents. In discovery, we are trained to ask every client if they have their estate documents in order and up to date. In many cases we find that this important planning element has been forgotten or neglected.

Confirm

Once we have shared our expertise with our clients and they have received a quote, proposal or illustration from us, then it is incumbent upon us to confirm that what we are recommending really does provide a solution for their needs and concerns. We do this by, once again, going over the reasons for the particular product or strategy and ensuring that the client is comfortable moving forward with the contract. I have learned over the years that confirmation doesn't mean asking for understanding. It may be that the client does understand the numbers, the strategy or the concept behind the plan we are putting together for them. But there is something more important that needs to be dealt with. In every case, before the client is finally obligated to make a payment, ask this question: *How does this feel to you?*

The way in which they answer this question is really the determining factor in confirming that our plan has provided them with the comfort and the solution that they were looking for. If, for some reason, the plan does not feel good to them, then it should be revisited. Clients who do not have confidence in a plan are the most likely to cancel it and try something different. However, if they feel secure in their knowledge and in the engagement process, it is more likely they will stick to the plan.

Follow-Up

We addressed follow-up in our previous chapter as it relates to a customer relationship management program (CRM) and being able to stay on top of our client engagement activities. As a part of client engagement, follow-up is the most important element apart from actually writing a contract. Follow-up is the key to business building in the financial services industry. Every successful advisor that I have met has a rigorous follow-up process to continue to engage their clients before, during and after a sale. It's important that we don't let any detail fall through the cracks when it comes to providing a high level of customer service. A strong follow-up process allows us to provide just such a service. Does this mean that we will never make a mistake or miss some task that we promise to our clients? Of course not. We are all human, and regardless of the systems that we put in place - mistakes are bound to happen. But it is our response to those mistakes that will set us apart from competition. Owning up to mistakes and addressing them quickly is as much a part of follow-up as sending thank you notes and updated investment statements. And it really doesn't matter whether you use a card box, a Rolodex, a spreadsheet, a sophisticated CRM program or a well-trained assistant; follow-up provides every single client with the knowledge that you are still engaged with their file and their concerns, and that you have not forgotten about them. This means that when the time comes for them to recommend you to one of their family, friends or colleagues you will be top of mind.

Finally, the reason that the National Best client engagement program is a circle of words is because, in the end, after our process is complete, we circle back to the beginning. Once we have onboarded a new client who has experienced our engagement program, we send them a thank you note, a token of our appreciation. So, there we are – back to *appreciation*. And now the cycle starts all over again, but instead of a sales cycle it is a customer service cycle.

Conclusion

So now we have developed a 1-Year goal using the famous SMART goal technique, and we have a client engagement system that will help us grow our business throughout the coming year. Although, in our industry, our primary goal is gross revenue numbers, the same technique could be used for any other annual goal that is important to your business. You might break a goal down into a certain number of clients in a target market. Although this would not represent a direct revenue number, it may be the quantity and quality of client that you will need to reach your target goal. No matter. We now have a way to track our production numbers and record any variance. But just keeping track is not enough. We also need to analyze, and for that we do the 3-Month Review.

Immediate Action Steps:

- Book a time in your calendar in the next month to write down your minimum, target, and outrageous annual goals for your business. Ensure you will have at least an hour of uninterrupted time. This may be scheduled at the same time as your business planning session, or a week or two later as part of the regular business-planning sessions that you have scheduled. You will want to ensure that you have your dream board, vision and mission statements, and your 3-year business plan with you to inspire you. *Schedule it now.*

- Text or email a trusted friend or colleague about your intention to spend this time setting your annual goals. *Do it now.*

- Download the annual goals worksheet and save it to your device. Have a quick look at the questions (also listed in the chapter above) and write down the names of any prospects and referral sources that come to mind. This will help you get started when you sit down to build the full list. *Do it now.*

https://mailchi.mp/93c0d198a165/8-step-dream-business-plan-worksheet

Step 5. The 3-Month Review

Every publicly traded company on the TSX or the Dow Jones industrial average is required to report quarterly earnings to their shareholders. This means they must review their business processes and their financials in order to fully inform their stakeholders. If this is a normal business practice of large successful companies, why would we think it would be any different for our small business?

In our 8-Step Dream Business Plan, the 3-Month Review is used to ensure that we are still on course and heading for that island paradise on the horizon. It is very easy to veer off course without a recalibration of our business plan on a regular basis.

Garbage In, Garbage Out – The Joy of Data Input

The 3-Month Review is all about data. Without the orderly collection of information, we would really have very little to review on a quarterly basis. For instance, if we only reviewed our 1-Year goal, that is, our annual revenue target, then we would be done in a matter of minutes. Since we have already implemented a spreadsheet solution to track our revenue streams, we have a running total that shows our gross revenue variance. By simply adding up all our business expense receipts and subtracting it from our gross revenue, we have our quarterly profit numbers. Now we know if we are on track to hit our 1-Year goal and if we can expect a profit or a loss based on our last three months of activity. You can see that the accurate collection of our revenue and expenses is the key to this analysis.

But this is just the tip of our analysis iceberg. There is much more to the 3-Month Review than simply crunching numbers. We need to dig deeper to find out exactly where our numbers came from and if we need to make changes to our plan to either increase, decrease or do away with the activities that contributed to that data. And we can't do that unless we have collected the right data diligently. This is one of the reasons that we stress the need for a *rigorous* CRM program and the use of spreadsheets for number crunching. Without accurate information our data analysis may be a foolhardy exercise. I have a friend who is a fantastic bookkeeper. She has a motto – Helping You Manage What You Measure. So, the question becomes exactly what should we measure so that we can better manage it?

Hey – Where Do You Come From?

I like to think of the 3-Month Review like meeting a new acquaintance for the first time. Developing a new relationship is all about curiosity. We are intrigued by this new individual and we would like to learn more about them. So, we ask them questions. And as they answer our questions, we begin to fill in all the blanks about their background and personality. In some ways, the 3-Month Review is about renewing your relationship with your business on a quarterly basis.

What are some of the questions that you might want to ask in your business?

- *Where did my revenue come from?*

- *What was the product mix?*

- *Which product created the most revenue and which the least?*

- *What were the source of my prospects?*

- *How much time did I spend on each prospect/new client?*

- *What percentage of my closed revenue came from existing clients versus new prospects?*

- *Which sales and marketing strategies worked, and which failed?*

- *Given the analysis of these numbers what should I change?*

You can see that these questions relate almost entirely to numbers. We start with an analysis of numbers since, as a responsible business owner, we must face them head-on. To face the numbers means to seek the truth. It does not serve our business, our clients or our colleagues to pretend we are successful when, in fact, our business requires an upgrade and a makeover. The concept of *"fake it 'til you make it"* may be valid in some industries, but in financial services our clients cannot afford to be underserved because of our lack of knowledge or resources. New advisors should always be leaning heavily on their managers, trainers and more experienced colleagues. And above all, we must be honest with ourselves when it comes to our business success. The 3-Month Review is all about honesty. One thing we can be sure of is that the numbers don't lie. Let's embrace our data and enjoy the fact that we have collected information that is going to help us grow and improve.

Sussing out the source of our revenue is a great place to start our 3-Month Review. By doing an analysis of our accounts receivable (commission statements for advisors) we can quickly see if our income source derives from existing clients or from new prospects. Typically, we market differently to these two groups. It's important to analyze our marketing efforts in either case.

We may have sent out an email blast to our current clients with a request to refer us to others in their network who could benefit from our services. If we have kept track of those referrals in our CRM program, then we can calculate our return on investment for having made that marketing decision. Alternatively, if we have sent out thank you notes to every single prospect that we bumped into at networking events, and have kept track of those business cards, then we can calculate our rate of return for that activity. It is our ability to be able to not only track the source of our income, but understand what sort of sales or marketing efforts produce the result that will allow us to move our business forward profitably. Obviously, if we have spent a lot of time and money at networking events, collected many cards, made many follow-up calls but produced very few results versus a large portion of our income coming from client referrals, then at least a surface analysis tells us we might want to direct less time and resources to particular networking events and direct more focused communication to our current client list. This is just an example. It might be that both activities produced an equal amount of revenue, so now we must dive deeper. We need to look at the cost in terms of time and money to produce the same amount of revenue.

You may have noticed that we have mentioned time as important data to track. The amount of time spent on any activity is important to record. Many professionals who work based on an hourly rate timestamp their files as a matter of course, otherwise they would have no accurate way to bill their clients. Although some financial advisors work on a fee-for-service basis and charge an hourly rate, the vast majority are commission-based and are not required to track hours. However, this is a mistake if we want to analyze our quarterly results. It is one thing to understand where our revenue comes from, but it is equally important to understand how much time it took to produce the result from each of our income sources. As an example, it may have taken us five hours to set up a corporate critical illness policy for a business owner that produced $5000 in revenue. It may have also taken us five hours to help a young family set up term policies to cover their mortgage producing $800 in commissionable earnings.

On the surface it appears as if we should be focusing more on business owners. This may be true, but once again, we need to dig a bit deeper in order to have a complete analysis. If the time you spent marketing to the business community in order to acquire the business client was ten times the cost of acquiring the young family, then that also must be considered. Also, if we are working in a team environment, it may be the case that we are better off to refer the young family to a junior advisor who we can supervise and share commission with rather than spend the full 5 hours in the family market. You can see how having accurate time data is important in our analysis. And perhaps our marketing efforts only produce one business owner per month as a prospect but 10 families, then we must be careful not to forsake one market for another unless we really are in a time crunch that does not allow us to serve all our prospects. Ultimately, that is the goal of our efforts – to become too busy to handle all our sales activities on our own.

Here is a sample from our 3-Month Review tab on our 8-Step Dream Business Plan spreadsheet:

Where did my revenue come from?

Referrals - Clients, Partners (internal, external)	17%
Marketing - Ads, Social Media, Mail Outs, Drop offs etc.	3%
Team Production - which team members - same breakdown as above	17%
Mining client list	63%
Total	**100%**

This is clearly a broad analysis and requires a deep dive in order for us to recommend any changes or adjustments to our business plan. One thing we can tell, though, is that our physical marketing efforts don't seem to be paying off. Does this mean we should stop purchasing ads, sending out social media messages or doing mail drops? That very well may be the case. But until we do further analysis, we can't be sure that the marketing dollars spent in these areas did not provide some value.

In financial services, particularly in the Life Insurance industry, we have a vast array of products that we can use to help our clients. In other businesses, this might represent different SKUs or different types of consulting work. It's important for us to understand which of the SKUs, units, or services produced the greatest revenue in our 3-Month Review. We use our spreadsheets and our CRM program to gather the data we need in order to determine our product mix. Once again, here is an example of a breakdown from our business plan spreadsheet:

Product Mix

Life Insurance	Term	25%
	Whole Life	35%
	Universal Life	0
Critical Illness Insurance		5%
Disability Insurance		8%
Health Spending Account		3%
Long-Term Care Insurance		
Exempt Market Dealer		
Segregated Funds		24%
Annuities		
Group Benefits/ Group Retirement		
Travel Insurance		
		100%

In the case above, it is clear that most of our revenue came from life insurance products. In fact, whole life provided us with almost one third of our revenue in total. Once again, more analysis is required. Each of these abbreviations can be further broken down into more specific products if we so choose. Notice how the life insurance products are broken out into the 3 basic types of life insurance in Canada: term, whole life, and universal life. But each of those categories could be further broken down if we wanted to do a deep dive analysis. As an example, term policies could be divided into the length of the term – 10-year term, 20-year term, 30-year term, term to age 100 etc. In addition, the whole life item could be further broken into participating whole life and non-participating whole life. Each time we take a magnifying glass to our data we gain a better understanding of where our revenue comes from and how we can derive income streams based on this analysis.

Next, we may want to look at where our prospects came from. We can look at all of the closed business in the quarter and for each commission paid we can make a list of the original prospect source. This is what it might look like in our spreadsheet:

| Original Prospect source | | | | | | | |
Networking	Trade Show	Biz Group	TEAM	Client Referral	Trail/ Renewal	Internal Referral	Bonus Pool
$336.61	$742.72		$35.00		$2,566.00	$1,412.78	$1,219.90
$1,706.00			$654.36		$3,325.73	$679.00	
$182.78			$1,050.00			$176.25	
$1,766.12		-$568.62	$461.00			$520.00	
$1,064.59			$325.00			$357.00	
$41.00			$1,224.00			$643.75	
$574.82						$486.39	
$5,671.92	$742.72	-$568.62	$3,749.36	$0.00	$5,891.73	$4,275.17	$1,219.90

Now we can see where each piece of closed business came from originally. When we begin to compare these numbers with our product mix, we start to gain insights into which products and activities have been working for our business. It will also show us where we've had some failures. Once again, this does not mean we have to make wholesale changes to our plan, it means that we need to draw conclusions that lead us to good business decisions.

In this example, we see that our networking efforts paid off quite handsomely over the quarter, our share of team revenue is also significant, and our internal referrals were also lucrative. You can see that the Biz Group column was a negative number. In our industry this represents a commission chargeback. If the client cancels a life insurance policy within the first two years, then the insurance company will claw back our commission on a 24-month prorated basis. So, does this mean we should resign from our business breakfast club? It is certainly something to consider, given the statistics of the last quarter. However, if we do an analysis of the last two quarters and go back as far as one year, it turns out that our revenue generated was significant. Our breakfast business group provided us with almost 25% of our annual revenue. In this case, the negative number represents an anomaly, but is something to be aware of, and perhaps to bring up with some of our club executive members. But, given our overall analysis, it is still not enough to have us quit the club.

With regard to our excellent networking results, we need to drill deeper to discover which of the events produced the most revenue. We may find that we went to 10 networking events over the quarter, but only two of them produced these results. We need to determine if they were one-offs, or if we've produced results because of attending these events time and again. If it does appear that these particular networking events produce good results, then we may want to adjust our focus, find more events like these and attend fewer events that produced no results.

We are now getting to the stage where our 3-Month Review can take on a life of its own. Once we have enough data and information on our spreadsheets, we can begin to cross-reference our analyses and start to draw some very specific conclusions about our activities.

As an example, we might find that one of our successful networking events produced our two largest commission opportunities and they were both business owners. Also, upon further examination we discovered that in both cases the product was a corporate split dollar critical illness strategy. Based on this analysis, we might build an initiative into our plan to attend more networking events of a similar nature and to ask our two new clients where they like to network. After all, networking is really about finding the events where your people hang out.

Another interesting aspect of reviewing our revenue origins is our trail/renewal income. In the financial services industry, most providers pay an ongoing income to the advisors to maintain their relationship with their clients. This ensures that the advisors will continue to provide information and ongoing help to customers of insurance and investment companies. It also provides advisors with a form of annuity that can allow them, at some point, to retire or semi-retire and develop a succession plan. By reviewing the source of the trail/renewal income, we can zero-in on strategies that enhance these results and ensure that our marketing efforts are directed toward clients that we want to build up in our book of business. This is another way to focus on specialization and higher levels of competence.

Finally, when we review our team results, we notice that it represented a large portion of our income. Not only did we receive an override on the team members who were in our agency or for whom we are responsible for training, but many of our referrals came from inside our organization. Once again, I do encourage product specialization so that we can refer business to the appropriate specialists and provide the best to our clients. These numbers help us to focus on our teammates who are clearly working with us. It is natural that we will want to reciprocate and to learn more about their specialty. With regard to our team overrides, it's important to focus on the team members that are doing well so we can continue to encourage their growth, and to ensure that the members who are struggling get the kind of attention and support they need to achieve their minimum targets.

What Worked and What Didn't

The ultimate goal of our 3-Month Review and the analysis of our data is to reveal the activities and strategies that worked in our business and those that did not. This is the time for true business honesty. If, in the face of numbers that prove our plan is not working, we make no changes, then we are wasting our time. The 3-Month Review puts a demand for improvement into our planning. The complete process should look like this:

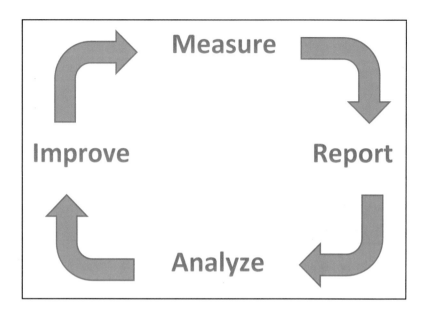

As an example, we may have come to the following conclusions regarding our analysis:

1. RRSP season provided our biggest gain.

2. This was achieved by mining our current client list, then doing an RRSP email blast.

3. We got more people out to an event dinner using proper follow-up.

4. We acquired only one new business client with a total of 35 calls.

5. We paid for a mailing list and did a mail out that did not produce significant results. In response, we might take the following steps to drive improvement:

   I. Follow-up with our RRSP clients for other business and referrals

II.   Increase the number of business owner calls to 70 next quarter

III.   Review our paid marketing approach and stop ads and mail outs for now

IV.   Do more direct drops to targeted clients

V.   Review with team members the upcoming quarter and coordinate efforts

In this case, we have decided to keep doing activities that have produced good results, to stop activities that produced disappointing results and to double our efforts marketing to a specific client – business owners. However, it's important to consider carefully how we plan to segment that target market. The one new client that we did acquire may give us a clue to a market vertical or to a specific industry that is receptive to our services. All this detailed analysis must be considered if we are to make changes that improve our 8-Step Dream Business Plan and help us achieve our goals. Depending on the size of your business and the size of your goals, the 3-Month Review could take a few hours or a few days. If you are going to include team members, then you may want to consider a weekend retreat, off-site, so that everyone can focus on the data and introduce ideas for improvement.

Spreadsheet Training - Graphing - Data Input

We cannot stress enough the importance of correct data input. However, we understand that not everyone is adept at using spreadsheets or CRM programs. If you or your team members lack skills using these tools, then a formal training program may be in order. Spreadsheet training is by far the easiest skill to acquire. There are courses online that can be accessed free of charge. The Calgary Public Library, for example, provides excellent courses on all Microsoft Office products as a part of free membership with your library card. Once your team is up to speed and comfortable using spreadsheets, teammates will gravitate naturally toward the kind of data input, reporting, analysis and improvement process that fits their business plan. As an example, many people respond better to graphical information rather than columns of numbers. If this is the case, then the spreadsheet allows them to produce graphs and pictograms to help them better understand the data being analyzed. An example might look like this:

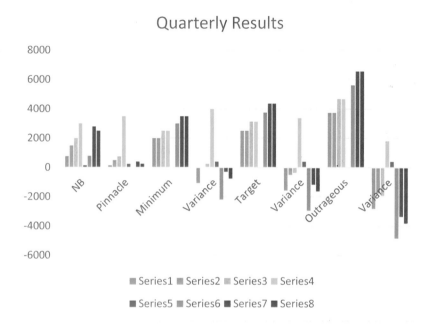

The visual representation of the data may be just what it takes to provide a teammate with insights that will help them make positive changes.

Working with a comprehensive CRM program is a bit different. Typically, it requires more intense training and a complete dedication to making use of it as a marketing, sales and customer service tool. However, as we have mentioned, being able to access information quickly and easily and respond to your market in a timely fashion, with accuracy and precision, will improve your overall results and make your book of business much more marketable when the time comes to look at succession.

Conclusion

Now that we have set sail using our 8-Step Dream Business Plan to develop our 10-Year Dream, our 5-Year Vision, 3-Year Plan, and our 1-Year Goal, it is our 3-Month Review that will keep us on course. Like all sailors, we must be constantly vigilant with regard to the waves, the wind and the weather. If we are to reach our island paradise on the horizon, we need to make regular adjustments as we plot our course.

Here are some questions we might ask ourselves at the end of every business quarter:

- *Steady as she goes? Is everything on track as we have planned and predicted?*

- *Trim the sails, alter the course? Should we make any minor adjustments to keep us on track?*

- *Change the course altogether? Is it time to abandon our original plan and try something new?*

Whatever our conclusions, it is the process of measuring, reporting, analyzing and implementing improvements that will ultimately get us to our destination.

Immediate Action Steps:

- Book a time in your calendar to do your quarterly reviews 3, 6, 9 and 12 months from now. You will need at least an hour or two depending on how detailed you want the analysis to be. *Schedule it now.*

- Text or email a trusted friend or colleague about your intention to spend these times doing your quarterly reviews. *Do it now.*

- If you have team members or employees that you want to participate in these quarterly reviews, notify them *now* with a calendar invite, email or text.

- Download the quarterly review worksheet and save it to your device. Have a quick look at the questions (also listed in the chapter above) and take note of what information you will require and where you will get it (e.g., your accountant, your bank statements, your commission statements, etc.). This will prepare you for your next quarterly review. *Do it now.* https://mailchi.mp/93c0d198a165/8-step-dream-business-plan-worksheet

Step 6. The 1-Month Schedule

"How did it get so late so soon?"
– *Dr. Seuss*

"A plan is what, a schedule is when. It takes both a plan and a schedule
to get things done."
– *Peter Turla*

The 1-Month Schedule is all about our business calendar. What is it filled with?

Whether you call it your scheduler, day timer, diary, appointment book or journal, whatever medium you use to book and track your daily activities, it must be filled every month. Not just filled out but filled to the brim with stuff to do. You might say that is an impossibility – filling every waking moment in your calendar is ludicrous! What about rest, relaxation, family time, vacations and other personal activities? Of course, we consider personal time important to a balanced life. But it must be scheduled, too. Remember, without data to track our time and measure our efficiency, we will not be able to report accurate information when it comes time to do our 3-Month Review. We need to know how we have spent our time in any given month. That includes personal time.

Too many self-employed individuals tend to leave personal and family time behind as they struggle with building their business. Their business calendar takes over. That is why we like to call our calendar the 1-Month Schedule. It should include our personal and family time as well as our business appointments, reminders and tasks. In fact, as we begin to construct a schedule using our calendar, we should begin with family time first. Start by filling in any time slots that are truly devoted to family or personal events that cannot be altered. These might include:

- Religious Practices

- Regular Workouts or Sports

- Child Care

- Date Nights

- Vacations

- Annual Family Events

- Volunteer or Charity Events

- Home Projects

I use a digital calendar (Outlook that syncs with my Gmail calendar) so it is very easy to schedule regular events for an entire calendar year. I can fill my calendar in minutes simply by making the activity a recurring event. Even if you have a paper-based calendar, I still recommend taking the time to go through the entire year and make sure you block out all of the personal time that cannot be devoted to building your business. The reason we do this is primarily psychological. For most new business owners and entrepreneurs there will always be activities that we will put on the back burner, particularly when they are important but not urgent. In business, we are often caught in the cycle of dealing with crises that divert our attention from critical long-term strategies that, although vital for growth, do not require our energy in the moment. One of the ways that business owners excuse themselves from these important tasks is to invoke the unalterable family event.

"I'm sorry, Bill, but I simply can't make that meeting on Friday, my wife is in Edmonton visiting her sister and I must take the kids to daycare."

"I just can't sit down with that client today since it is the only chance I will get to mow the lawn before we leave on vacation."

"I know I should sit down and get the changes done to my website, but the Olympics are on and I want to watch the diving event."

All these excuses to not attend to business will seem very valid to some people and very lame to others. It is not really a matter of judgement but, rather, a matter of scheduling. The bottom line is that if these events had been pre-booked into your calendar, then the important business events could have been scheduled at other available times. Instead, we often use family events that we know will occur and that we could make accommodation for as an excuse to bail on our business - *(I knew my wife was visiting her sister a month ago; I can get the neighbor's kid to mow the lawn while we vacation; the Olympics TV schedule is published months in advance)*.

By making a point of scheduling all our activities into our calendar, we can make sure that our important business activities do not get pushed off, downgraded or forgotten altogether. Of course, there will be legitimate crises that happen that will require us to make scheduling changes. There is nothing wrong with that at all. We just want to make sure that the deferral of important activities and the need to reschedule appointments are due to legitimate reasons and not to a lack of planning.

Now that we have all our family and personal scheduling in place, it's time to get down to business. How do we begin to fill in our business schedule? What sorts of activities, reminders and tasks should be included in our calendar?

For most independent advisors in the financial services industry, the answer is actions that lead to production.

Actions That Lead to Production

If the entries in the business section of your calendar do not lead directly to production, then you need to ask *why?* Ask yourself:

- *Why am I going to this networking event?*

- *Why am I writing this blog?*

- *Why am I posting on Facebook?*

- *Why am I spending time to build a profile on LinkedIn?*

- *Why am I going to this team meeting?*

The question that should come up more often than any of the others is:

How can I help this important client or prospect?

This last question triggers all of the activity that leads to success in our industry. In fact, this is the question that drives success in most businesses today. Without successful service to our clients we have no business to speak of. The acquisition, engagement and loyalty of clients who find value and success using our products or services should be the focus of virtually every calendar entry in our business schedule. If you have an entry in your business calendar and you cannot draw a line directly from that activity to writing a contract, you may need to reconsider.

Of course, there are some activities that are required parts of our business but don't lead directly to production. In the financial services sector, maintaining our licensing through Continuing Education (CE) credits is one of those activities. In Alberta, in order to retain our life and our accident and sickness licenses, we require 15 CE credits per license. A CE credit translates roughly into one hour of education time. That means that in order to retain both of our licenses we need to schedule at least 30 hours of training per year into our calendar. If we include travel time or other preparation, then the fulfilment of our CE credits consumes an entire work week per year. In most cases, these activities will not lead directly to production, however, we understand that as a regulatory requirement we can write no business without being licensed. So, in spite of the fact that it may not seem like a productive activity, it is necessary.

There could be other activities like continuing education that may not result directly in writing new business but may indirectly contribute to our business development. Some of these might include:

- In-house training programs

- Business coaching or mastermind groups

- New networking events

- Management meetings

- Customer service activities

- Vacations (need to recharge and stay focused)

Obviously, some of the items in the list are necessary to our business, such as customer service activities. Although it may not seem like the kind of activity that would lead directly to new business, often, if handled correctly, a high level of service to our current clients leads to referrals or to additional business from the same client. This is a good example of an activity that could lead to new business indirectly. Some of the other activities may not seem quite so obvious. At first, it may seem like a vacation could hardly lead to new business. But without some form of regular relaxation and time away from our business, it is difficult to stay energetic and focused and, in some cases, take the opportunity to step back and look at our business from an outside perspective. Often, this perspective can lead us to some interesting conclusions. Time away from the daily grind can provide us with a chance for more creative thought that could lead to ideas that, indeed, generate increased production.

Let's not dismiss all activity that does not lead directly to production, but let's keep tabs on those calendar entries that may seem important or urgent but are really just a distraction from our primary aim, which is to achieve our 1-Year Goal. And in order to do that, we need to be sitting down in front of prospects or clients on a regular basis. Our planning up to this point should have told us how many contracts we will have to write in any given week or month to achieve our goals. I am not going to dwell on the numbers that are required to produce those results in this book. Everyone in our industry knows that if you don't pick up the telephone and talk to people, there is no way forward. Our calendar has to be filled with appointments that result in business. We need to be talking with people who are in need of our services, and in order to do that, we need to have a list of names.

Does your calendar look like this?

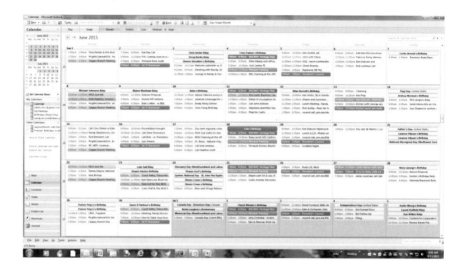

Or like this?

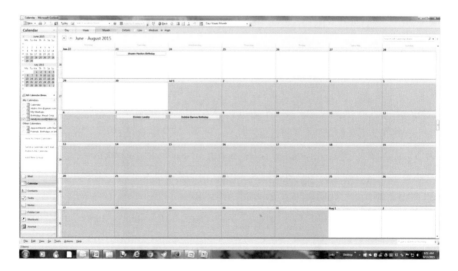

Every new advisor in the financial services industry is asked to write down a list of their closest friends, relatives, acquaintances and colleagues. The financial services industry is a people business and without a list of people to talk to, a new advisor has nowhere to start. Typically, new advisors are asked to make appointments with their nearest and dearest, not so much to sell to them, but rather to introduce themselves as an advisor. These initial meetings are often used as field training exercises by their managers or trainers. The hope is that their inner network, once informed about the new advisor's business, will be willing to refer people from their extended network.

Remember that in our 3-Year Plan we have also tried to develop our natural markets. Natural markets can generate valuable lists based on their specific focus. For some new advisors, their religious community might be a natural market. For others, it could be their cultural community, and for advisors who have come from the corporate world it might be their business connections that are a natural fit for their business plan. In any case, the lists that we create are the basis upon which we fill our calendar with productive appointments.

I teach a workshop on how to build a referral network and how to develop productive relationships at business events. As an exercise, I often tell new advisors to leave their business cards at home when they go to a networking event. This is to remind them that their goal is to collect cards, not to hand out cards. Any networking event with more than a dozen attendees should allow a new advisor the opportunity to collect at least four or five cards. Each individual requires prompt and considered follow-up. When approached correctly, every card should represent a future appointment in your business calendar. This means that if you have a goal of ten new appointments per week, then attending to business networking events that will generate five new contacts is one way of developing an ongoing list.

Harwinder Kang, the president of National Best, often reminds us of an exercise that he likes to employ in order to check on the productivity of his schedule. For two weeks he writes down every single activity he does every day. That means that if he stops to make a cup of tea and takes a 15-minute break, he records it. If you want to get creative with this exercise, then you can color code different activities. As an example, you could make client appointments green and personal activities orange. You could make networking events purple and new prospect calls blue. We could make any appointment that involved writing a contract the color red. We can now go back over two weeks of our calendar and see exactly where we have spent our time. Harwinder does this on a regular basis to ensure that he sees more productive colors than nonproductive colors. This kind of calendar self-assessment is an excellent way to make sure our time is well spent. We don't want our business activity to fool us. Just because we are busy and we fill our calendar with reminders, tasks and appointments, it does not mean that we are profitable. The ultimate goal of our 1-Month Schedule is to fill our lead funnel and our sales pipeline.

Lead Funnel and Sales Pipeline

In our 1-Month Schedule, all of our efforts should in some way feed our lead funnel. Funnels have a wide brim for a very good reason. It ensures that we can catch as much of the liquid possible when we are pouring into a vessel, without losing any of it. Our lead funnel is built for the same purposes. We want to draw in potential clients, potential recruits, potential referral partners or even colleagues with whom we can build a working relationship. We use our CRM program to keep track of our leads as well as our clients and our new business. Our CRM program must work in concert with our 1-Month schedule, and the best CRM programs will typically sync with Outlook, Gmail or other standard digital calendars and email clients. This is technology that I would definitely recommend learning about and implementing into your business.

Once leads have been recognized as actionable, they need to be put into a call cycle. If they are a prospective client, then we need to stay in touch with them until they are ready to move forward with their financial planning. Every prospective client will have a different timeline when it comes to making a decision about your products or services. So, they need to be entered into your calendar in a way that serves their agenda. You simply must ask them when you should be in contact with them in the future. Whatever that date is should be scheduled and followed up on like clockwork. If you truly care about helping your potential clients, you must show them that you listen to their requests and you respond on time.

Once a lead has decided to make a buying decision, we move them into our sales pipeline. The sales pipeline represents our revenue and cash flow, and it's by assisting our potential clients through this pipeline that we provide them with valuable service and advice. In any given sales process, from the first call until final delivery, there are key points in the process that should be scheduled and in our calendar. After having written a contract, I make a point of scheduling a follow up call with the client within a week to report on progress. The progress report allows the client to stay involved with the sales pipeline activity. And as we have discussed, after sales, customer service can also be scheduled. These are some of the tasks that can fill out our calendar in the spaces between our appointments. Again, our CRM program allows us to build action plans that will automatically remind us when we need to get back in touch with a client, send out a follow up or reminder, email or other communication. By automating our action plans we begin to fill our calendar with productive activity.

747 Club - Accountable Activity Plan

Being an entrepreneur or small business owner means having to be self-motivated. It means getting up every day and reviewing your 1-Month Schedule with the understanding that there is no guarantee of a pay cheque. And for individuals who are new to a business, it can seem even more daunting if there is no clear plan. In order to assist our new advisors at National Best, and particularly our part-time advisors, our leadership developed an accountability activity plan that we called the 747 Club.

Our President, Harwinder Kang, is a pilot and he liked to use the analogy of a plane taking off to explain to new advisors how they could expect their business to grow. From that analogy, we thought it would be fun to create some pins with wings on them that we can award to new advisors who completed the 747 activities. The concept behind the 747 Accountability Plan was fairly simple. In order to earn their wings, the advisor had to complete 7 activities per week for 7 weeks. We provided a list of productive activities that ranged from booking appointments, submitting business or filling out an nbNavigator Data Collection Sheet to simply attending training meetings. The 8th week is for relaxation and reflection. In addition to receiving your wings, you are given the opportunity to take a break and prepare for the next round of the 747 Club. Once again, we incorporated the plan directly into our 8-Step Dream Business Plan spreadsheet.

Like all programs that have been developed by National Best, the 747 Activity Plan was eventually expanded, and we began producing pins for the 757 Club and the 767 Club. These were simply programs that expanded the number of activities required and were geared more for full-time advisors. What we discovered, and what is, perhaps, self-evident, is that success in our business depends upon productive activity just like it does in virtually every business. The 747 Activity Plan promoted exactly the kind of activity needed to produce results. New advisors who took up the challenge to get their wings quickly were ultimately earning income before others who were not so keen to commit to the program immediately.

 **NATIONAL**
TOGETHER WE ARE THE BEST

Name: _____

Week #1   2   3   4   5   6   7

Start Date: _____

Report for week: _____

Completion Date: _____

Earn your wings and watch your business take flight!!

Track your business			Mon	Tue	Wed	Thu	Fri	Sat	Sun
Urgent	8	Client Appointments	2	0	1	3	2	0	0
& important	0	Qualified Referral to a Specialist	0	0	0	0	0	0	0
	0	New Business Submission Form	0	0	0	0	0	0	0
	0	nbNavigator	0	0	0	0	0	0	0
	0	Phone Calls	0	0	0	0	0	0	0
Still Important	0	Recruiting appointment	0	0	0	0	0	0	0
	0	Business Development/Community Event	0	0	0	0	0	0	0
	0	Business Building Coffee/Lunch	0	0	0	0	0	0	0
	0	Networking Event/Trade Show/Industry	0	0	0	0	0	0	0
	0	Attending an nbWorkshop	0	0	0	0	0	0	0
	0	Lead nbWorkshops	0	0	0	0	0	0	0
Not Urgent &	0	Mentor with an Associate (1 hr.) 1 each	0	0	0	0	0	0	0
Still Important	0	Lead Team Training	0	0	0	0	0	0	0
	0	Attended Online Training	0	0	0	0	0	0	0
	0	Attended nbSynergy or nbPower Team	0	0	0	0	0	0	0
	0	Attend Conferences /Convention	0	0	0	0	0	0	0
	0	Active Participation in nbProjects	0	0	0	0	0	0	0
	0	Leading nbPower Team	0	0	0	0	0	0	0
	0	NB Trainer, Management role	0	0	0	0	0	0	0
	0	Coaching	0	0	0	0	0	0	0
	0	Completing Academy Levels	0	0	0	0	0	0	0
	0	Achieving Next Promotion	0	0	0	0	0	0	0
	8	WEEKLY TOTAL	2	0	1	3	2	0	0

757 Goal (complete minimum **100** activites in **7** weeks)   767 Goal (complete minimum **150** activities in **7** weeks)

747 Goal (complete minimum 7 activities/week X 7 weeks = **49** activities)

Productive Time Management Yellow + Blue = Green $$$$	NBSF - New Business Submission Form
Safe Plan - NBSF immediately, S/B the largest amount of time	Rich Plan - What I do to build multiple streams of
Comfortable Plan - What I do that leads to NBSF in near future	income, systematize, secure & increase my business

 **NATIONAL**
TOGETHER WE ARE THE BEST

Track your business

Goals: How much do I want to make this week? _____

How many people do I want to help this week? _____

Results: How much did I make this week? _____

How many people did I help? _____

Business Submitted: _____ Type of Business: _____ # of Points: _____

Recruits: # of people I talked to about NB? _____ # of completed MAPs: _____

Leads - Referrals: # of Referrals: _____ # of Connections: _____

Connect: Networking Events _____ Calls: _____

Discover/: 1st appointments _____ 2nd appointments _____ nbNavigator _____

Share: 3rd Appointments _____ Follow-up _____ Client Review _____

Share: Group Presentations Workshops _____ # of Lunch & Learns _____

Confirm: Closing Business _____

Follow-up: Things to Complete _____

Appreciate: **Send Cards, Emails, Phone** _____

Conclusion

Our 1-Month Schedule is the revenue generator of our 8-Step Dream Business Plan. By ensuring that it is filled with productive activity, we can advance step-by-step toward our goals. By using our 3-Month Review to constantly improve our processes, our 1-Year Goal to assess our success and our 3-Year Plan to keep us on course, our 5-Year Vision and our 10-Year Dream will soon be in view. Our final two chapters, the 1-Week Focus and the 1-Day Task List, are really the ultimate generators of entries into our 1-Month Schedule. Let's see how they fit into our plan!

Immediate Action Steps:

- Book a time in your calendar to do your monthly scheduling. You will need at least half an hour to ensure that you are setting up your schedule according to your priorities and to ensure you are on track to achieve your 10-Year Dream, your 5-Year Vision, your 3-Year Plan and your annual goal. *Schedule this recurring appointment now.*

- Text or email a trusted friend or colleague about your intention to spend these times setting up your monthly schedule. *Do it now.*

- If you have family members, team members or employees that need to be consulted when setting your monthly schedule, consider inviting them to these sessions or at least getting the information from them in advance.

- Download the monthly schedule worksheet and save it to your device. Make a quick list of the types of activities you want to schedule (e.g., family time, recreation / exercise / hobbies / special work projects). This will prepare you for your next monthly scheduling session. *Do it now.*

  https://mailchi.mp/93c0d198a165/8-step-dream-business-plan-worksheet

Step 7. The 1-Week Focus

"When walking, walk. When eating, eat."

- Zen proverb

"One look at an email can rob you of 15 minutes of focus. One call on your cell phone, one tweet, one instant message can destroy your schedule, forcing you to move meetings, or blow off really important things like love, and friendship."
- Jacqueline Leo

As entrepreneurs and business owners, a myriad of demands are often put on us on a weekly basis. In the world of financial services, particularly in the life insurance arena, there is a lot of paperwork and follow-up. As we begin to develop a book of business, those demands become greater and greater. There is a need to serve our current clients while, at the same time, acquiring new customers. We hope to keep on top of these demands by using our automated follow-up systems and our 1-Month Schedule. But there are also regulatory demands, supplier requests, new industry information that needs to be digested and fellow advisors that need training and support. In this kind of hectic environment, it is very easy to let the week get away from us when it comes to completing important projects or vital tasks. Thus, the need for the 1-Week focus.

At the beginning of every work week it is important to focus on a specific task or project that would significantly advance your business if it were completed. As we mentioned in the last chapter, we need to fill our calendar with productive activity. The weekly focus is an excellent way to fill in any gaps that we have in our schedule. The specific focus could be almost any undertaking that will contribute to our overall goal. This might include:

- a phone zone (a specific time to make numerous phone calls)

- writing scripts that we can use during our phone zone

- writing a blog

- organizing our monthly newsletter

- updating our CRM program

- researching a company that we would like to call on

- organizing our filing system

- reading a book that will help us with self-development

- studying a product that we would like to specialize in

- meeting with colleagues to organize a seminar or workshop

- field training with the new recruit

In each case, the focus for the week should be something we *truly* want to get done and it sits at the top of our calendar every day until it is achieved. We may have to devote several hours during the week to achieve this important pursuit. But, whether we are full-time or part-time, we must make the 1-Week Focus the priority in our calendar.

Even if we follow the 747 Accountable Activity Plan, which allows us one week every two months to take a break, this will still leave us with up to 40 weeks of intense targeted activity. Any business owner can be successful if they can make this a cornerstone of their weekly schedule. The 1-Week focus becomes the bedrock upon which the rest of our week is built.

One of our founders, Dr. Maria Lizak, spends every Sunday evening reviewing her previous week and making plans for the coming week. Even with a busy home life she tries to find some quiet time after the kids are in bed to look ahead and develop a focal point for the next 7 days. Consider the following:

- What do you need to achieve this week?

- How does achieving it relate to your goals and plan?

- How will you stay focused?

This last question is of the utmost importance. When I decided to write this book, I estimated that I could complete it in approximately three months if I devoted three hours per week solely to this one task. I will freely admit that I work in spurts. I tend to be easily distracted by almost anything that crops up in my email, my social media or paperwork on my desk that needs to be dealt with. So, I had to think carefully about which days and which hours I would devote to my writing.

At first, I thought that working on the book late in the evening would be the answer, but I quickly discovered that my devotion to my favorite television shows got in the way. If I did not have client appointments or training sessions, my evenings were a time to wind down, relax in my La-Z-Boy, and let go of the stresses of the day. Even though I believed I had the time if I made a few adjustments, it did not work. I had to rethink my strategy.

After some soul searching, I had to admit that I had become a morning person. Even after years of being a night owl in the music industry, and generally staying up quite late most nights, I got the majority of my urgent and important work done between 8:00 a.m. and 1:00 p.m. daily - then a break and some clean up in the late afternoon. Of course, some days were all out and some were more laid back, but I seemed to have the most focus in the morning. Also, I had committed to a strength and conditioning regimen with a personal trainer on Mondays, Wednesdays and Fridays at 6:00 a.m. and an aerobics circuit on Sundays at 11:00 a.m. This meant that during the week I was at my desk by 7:30 a.m. after training. I made the decision that I would write between 7:30 a.m. and 9:00 a.m. But that was not the full commitment. I vowed not to open my email, my social media, my snail mail or work on a client file until 9:00

a.m. The hour and a half between workout and starting my business day was to be devoted only to writing.

Did it work? I leave it to you, gentle reader, to render that judgement.

There will always be important anchors in your calendar, some that occur weekly. The 1-Week Focus should be one of them. As noted above, my workout sessions anchor three of my mornings per week. Our Tuesday evening training and cross-Canada webinar is another anchor. On Thursday mornings I attend a weekly business networking group. There may also be personal or family anchors that act as pivotal weekly events such as Sunday dinner or date night. These anchors become important when it comes to the 1-Week Focus, since we need to ensure that the time devoted to the important work of the focus is not easily interrupted. The pre-scheduled events must not supersede the 1-Week Focus, since we have made a commitment to our 8-Step Dream Business Plan that this job must get done. So, carefully consider the time slots that you will use for the 1-Week Focus, as I had to do in writing this book. If you get it wrong, you may find yourself carrying over the task week after week, but if you get it right, your business could benefit beyond measure.

Conclusion

Business owners and solopreneurs are, by nature, extremely busy. It is often difficult to maintain focus for any length of time when they are trying to juggle four or five important matters whilst wearing two or three different hats. In the next chapter, we will review some of the daily activities that will help us deal with the many urgent matters that arise in our business. By developing our 8-Step Dream Business Plan, our goal is to organize, systematize and automate our business so that we free up the necessary time we need to devote to our important short-term and long-term projects. The 1-Week focus is our reminder to get done that which is both urgent and important.

Immediate Action Steps:

- Open your calendar now and schedule a recurring 1-hour time block to set your weekly focus. During that hour every week, you will set your focus for the upcoming week and schedule time to do it. *Do it now.*

- Download the weekly focus worksheet and save it to your device. This will ensure you are ready for your first weekly focus session. *Do it now.* https://mailchi.mp/93c0d198a165/8-step-dream-business-plan-worksheet

- Make a quick list of tasks or projects that would significantly advance your business if they were completed. This list will help when you are setting your weekly focus. *Do it now.*

- Share this list with a trusted friend or colleague. *Do it now.*

Step 8. The 1-Day Task List

"The most efficient way to live reasonably is every morning to make a plan of one's day and every night to examine the results obtained."

– Alexis Carrel

The Man in the Mirror

Harwinder Kang, the president of National Best, has a little story that he likes to tell new recruits to our company. He says:

"Every morning I wake up and prepare for the coming day. Just like everyone else I must brush my teeth, wash my face, comb my hair (at least back when I had hair) and get ready to face the day. It's at that point that I look at that man in the mirror and I say to him – it's up to you. The good things that will happen to you today are because you took action to do the right thing with a positive mindset. You cannot control what others do but you can control how you react to them. You are the pilot and if you want to take off today, it's time to go full throttle, lift off and fly. Follow your flight plan and you will arrive at your destination safe and sound. The man in the mirror is the key to your success."

Over the decades, I've read many books, watched many videos and attended many seminars on motivation, mindset and self-actualization. The self-help industry is rife with authors and speakers who will explain their "magic" techniques to achieve business or personal success. I've tried them all and I can tell you that I have found nothing to match the simple process of talking to the person in the mirror every morning. If you believe in the power of positive affirmation and every morning you say out loud positive statements that are supposed to set up your day, then say it to the person in the mirror. If you write down your 10-Year Dream and your 5-Year Vision and you want to remind yourself that they represent your *Why,* then paste them on the bathroom mirror and recite them every morning to that familiar reflection. All you have to do is imagine that person in the mirror is the best version of yourself and you cannot help but have a good day.

Harwinder and Dr. Maria are the reason that I am in the financial services business today. Harwinder is a business freight train, a tremendous strategist and a leader with the highest emotional intelligence quotient of anyone I have ever met. Dr. Maria is a farm girl with five younger brothers, an intellectual (PhD in Psychology) turned business leader who lights up a room with positivity wherever she goes. Who wouldn't want to go into business with these two? When I look at the man in the mirror every morning, I tell him how lucky he is to have a wonderful business opportunity and amazing colleagues to help me build it.

So, this morning, what conversation are you having with that person in the mirror?

Get Action: With the Right Mindset

"Get action. Do things; be sane; don't fritter away your time; create, act, take a place wherever you are and be somebody; get action."

— *Theodore Roosevelt*

I love this Teddy Roosevelt quote. It is a stern reminder that nothing in our lives will happen until we get action. Certainly nothing is going to happen in your business until you take up the responsibilities and commitments that are built into your 8-Step Dream Business Plan. Just remember that the actions you take every day are getting you one step closer to your goals. Some days they will be baby steps and other days they will be giant leaps. A positive mindset is all that is required. It will allow you to take the failures, challenges and setbacks in stride. As long as we get action with the right mindset, we set ourselves up for success.

New advisors are often challenged by the many demands of our industry just as all entrepreneurs are challenged in their respective sectors. Sometimes it can be hard to decide what to do first in any given day. What is the most important task to accomplish? We have our weekly focus but what about today? How do we determine our focus for today? How do we triage the tasks on our 1-Day Task List?

I like to combine two elements to help advisors with these questions: The Eisenhower Matrix and Randy's 6 Daily Fundamentals.

The Eisenhower Matrix

The Eisenhower Matrix

	URGENT	NOT URGENT
IMPORTANT	**Q1** **DO NOW**	**Q2** **DECIDE WHEN TO DO IT**
NOT IMPORTANT	**Q3** **DELEGATE IT AWAY**	**Q4** **DELETE IT**

waitbutwhy.com

During the 2nd World War, Dwight D. Eisenhower was the Supreme Commander of the Allied forces. It was a daunting task, and Eisenhower had to make life and death decisions on a daily basis. He found that it became more and more difficult to focus on which tasks should be completed at any given time. This led him to invent his famous decision-making matrix – The Eisenhower Matrix.

As you can see from our graphic, the matrix is broken down into 4 quadrants based upon 4 simple questions with regard to a decision that has to be made. The questions are:

1. Is the Decision/Action Urgent?

2. Is the Decision/Action Important?

3. Is the Decision/Action Not Urgent?

4. Is the Decision/Action Not Important?

By asking these simple questions with regard to any decision he had to make, he could quickly delegate the it to one of the 4 quadrants. For instance, if your spouse were to go into labor, then the decision to go to the hospital would be important and urgent. That would place the decision into quadrant number 1 which says: *Do it now*. On the other hand, if your lawn needed to be cut but you suddenly had guests show up for dinner, then you have a decision which is important but not urgent. Thus, it will fall into quadrant 2, and we would simply have to reschedule our lawn trimming to another day. Can you think of some decisions that would fall into quadrant 3 and 4? In the next section we will see how we can build our daily task list and sort it by priority using Randy's 6 Daily Fundamentals and The Eisenhower Matrix.

Randy's Six Daily Fundamentals
Here are *Randy's 6 Daily Fundamentals*:

1. Write Business - Follow Up

2. Call a Client

3. Call a Prospect

4. Make a Call from Your List

5. Market or Network to Build a List

6. Study

As you can see, my very first fundamental is centered on making money. In the financial services industry, new advisors have to be writing business on an ongoing basis to survive. If they are not writing up an application, submitting an application or following up on an application, they will have no revenue in the pipeline. If they have no revenue, they will have to leave the business. Some models which allow part-time advisors might argue that it's okay if part-timers aren't producing as long as they are attending meetings, staying up to date with regulatory issues and learning about new products and strategies. I am not an advocate of this thinking, nor is the industry in general. Most recently, life insurance companies have placed minimum quotas into their contracting agreements. Time is precious in our short lives and there are lots of different careers and activities we could be doing. Clearly, if your efforts are not paying off, it is probably time to move on.

Remember how I mentioned in earlier chapters that, in our industry, payment is often deferred for several months? This is the reason that our pipeline must be filled with active applications. Until a financial advisor has built a sizable book of business, there is a need for ongoing transactions. Some businesses that have much larger transactions need to do them less frequently. The same could be said for financial services. Some advisors who target high net worth individuals may need to do fewer transactions to reach their 1-Year goal than a new advisor who is dealing in a middle-class market. It is just the reality of the business.

Since an advisor cannot survive without writing new business or following up on applications and delivering policies or investment statements, this becomes the number one activity on the 1-Day Task List. Why? Because according to The Eisenhower Matrix, this activity is both important and urgent. An application in process is of the utmost importance to the client and needs to be addressed immediately. To ensure this happens, we do not get paid until the processing is complete. Our current active files can also be sorted using the matrix, depending on where they are in the processing pipeline. If we have an appointment to write up an application with the client, that is clearly in quadrant 1. However, if we have just submitted an application, we know that it will be in the queue for, perhaps, a week or so and, although following up is important it, is not urgent - we can put that decision into quadrant 2. We can schedule a follow-up with the underwriter and report to our client at a later date.

Also, depending on our internal business model, we may have an assistant or office manager that will handle applications once they have been submitted. In this case, the application process is urgent, but it is not important to us personally, thus we can delegate it away according to quadrant 3. You can see how the combination of active business and The Eisenhower Matrix helps us quickly arrange our 1-Day Task List.

Note that follow-up is one of the key words in our first fundamental. This is because follow-up is essential, not only regarding ongoing applications, but also in communication with our clients. In order to provide a very high level of customer service we need to be in close communication with our clients, particularly during application processing. The essential dictum of the number one fundamental is: *serve clients – make money.*

Call a Client

What if our new advisor does not have any applications currently in the pipeline? Then our number 2 fundamental for our 1-Day Task List is to make a call to a client. As we have mentioned, customer service is the foundation for our business. We need to stay in touch with our clients to make sure that our decisions, with regard to their protection and their wealth, serve their needs on an ongoing basis. Just as important is making sure that they understand that we are available to help their loved ones with the same level of service. By staying in touch with our clients on a regular basis we make sure that any changes in their circumstances are reflected in their financial plan. When we do this, they are much more likely to refer us to their friends, family and colleagues. Also, their changing circumstances may demand a review of their financial plan and may open the door to new or additional strategies where our services are required. Once again, we can subscribe to The Eisenhower Matrix to decide which clients on our list need our attention immediately, which can be rescheduled to a later date or perhaps can be delegated to an assistant or an automated call back. So, if you are not writing business or in the process of following up on applications - *call a client.*

Call a Prospect

Now our new advisor comes to us and says, *"I have been in touch with all my clients in the last few weeks, so I have no one left to call."* In that case, it is time to call a prospective client. We simply go to our list of clients and prospective clients and make a call to set up an appointment. Remember, when it comes to prospective clients, all we are looking for is an appointment. We don't want to spend any length of time on the telephone trying to explain financial planning in any kind of detail. This is an activity that is best done face-to-face. And of course, we can perform triage on our list of prospective clients using the matrix. For example, if our best referral partner has provided us with the name of a prospect that has told us that they are looking for life insurance coverage before they fly to Australia on vacation next month, then they obviously fall into quadrant 1. On the other hand, if we make a call to a prospect and find that they are well insured, that they have a trusted advisor and they are not looking for a second opinion at this time, we might place them into quadrant 4. Notice that quadrant 4 tells us to delete this prospect. It might be that we want to keep the contact information of this prospect, but we definitely want to remove them from our sales cycle. So, it's not that we eliminated their information, rather, we simply eliminated them from our lead funnel and our sales pipeline. Calling a new prospect should probably occur every day unless we are so busy with business processing and attending to our current clients that we have no time. However, be warned – nothing lasts forever, and prospecting calls will always be important, if for no other reason than to replace the natural attrition that will occur in any book of business. If our 1-Day Task List does not have business to write or clients to call, then it's time to call a prospect.

Make a Call from Your List

Today, my recruit comes to me and tells me that they do not have any business to process, they don't have any clients to call and they don't have any clear prospects. What do they do now? Our 4th fundamental is to go to our list of potential prospects and pick some out in order to make phone calls for appointments. If our 1-Day Task List does not include a single phone call, then we have a problem. Our list should contain all our future potential clients. As I mentioned previously, almost all the business models in financial services require new advisors make a list of their closest contacts. Often, this is referred to as the Top 25 List. But that is just the start. There are other exercises in the industry that have the recruit go over a list of 100 different professions or relationships where they might find names of individuals that can go on the list.

When I teach my workshop on building referral networks, I ask the participants for the number of people they believe they are close to. Often, they mention 15 – 25 warm associations. Some social butterflies might say 50 dear friends and colleagues. Then I ask them to count the number of entries on their cell phone contact list. Typically, the lowest number that we find is around 100. The average is closer to 250. Suddenly, their eyes are opened to the actual size of their network. When we go to our call list, we should have at least 250 people or companies on the list. We can apply The Eisenhower Matrix, once again, to sort the list in terms of the urgency or importance of a follow-up call. The triage might be related to our overall target market, our weekly focus or just a name that pops up that is of interest. No business, no clients, no prospects means it's time to refer to our list and make some calls.

Market or Network to Build a List

I'm sure that by now you can see where this process is going. The 1-Day Task List is built around production. It does not mean we cannot have unproductive activities scheduled, but without specific tasks that result in revenue, our business will collapse. So, if we have exhausted the first 4 Fundamentals for any given day, it's our job to build up our list. Whether we build the list via some form of marketing campaign or simply by networking and collecting cards, our ultimate goal is to create productive activity. Most marketing experts will tell you that advertising builds brand awareness, but direct marketing and face-to-face meetings generate revenue. For most new advisors, networking represents the most effective and least costly means of building their list. And as always, we can use The Eisenhower Matrix to separate our lists into the various quadrants in order to determine who should be called first and how often. As an example, if we have targeted a large company with 500 employees as a prospect for group benefits, then they may fall into quadrant 1 as we gather information about them and find out who the decision-maker is in the organization. An important contact that we met at a business mixer may be a potential referral partner who runs an accounting firm. In this case, the call isn't urgent, but it is important, so we need to schedule our call for a future date when we can devote time to building that relationship. In some cases, we may want to do a mass marketing campaign, so we might purchase lists of companies or individuals, or we might hire a call centre to set up appointments for us. In other cases, lists can be collected at no cost from various public sources including business associations, public libraries, industry directories and government lists. However we go about building our call lists, the collection process should be targeted and focused on our market verticals. Almost every list will contain clients who are in need of our services and fit our target market perfectly. These are the ones that should be on our 1-Day Task List.

Study

There will come a day, no matter how excited and energetic we are about our business, that we will be tired of talking to people. Almost everyone, at some point, needs some alone time. Not just to recharge, but also to focus on working *on* our business rather than *in* it. But there may be days when we don't even want to work on our business, nor do we want to deal with clients, prospects, networking or looking at lists. But it is still a workday and we still need to get something done. We still need to put something on our 1-Day task list that is productive in some way, shape or form. *That's when we study.*

The key to making sure our 8-Step Dream Business Plan comes to fulfilment is by becoming ever better at what we do. By becoming experts in our field, we better serve our clients. By taking on the mantle of lifetime learning, we will make sure that we stay at the top of our game. How do we use The Eisenhower Matrix when it comes to study? There is virtually an infinite amount of information that is available to us with regard to our industry. The matrix can help us boil it down to those books, articles, seminars and webinars that relate most closely to our 3-Year Plan, our 1-Year Goal and our Weekly Focus. If we're going to take a break from people for a while, then let's study information that will help us build our business more quickly.

Conclusion

Every day we rise and go to work. Our 1-Day Task List helps us stay organized and accountable for what we do every day to build our business. An honest look in the mirror can go a long way to help us tackle our list and fulfil our potential.

Immediate Action Steps:

- Open your calendar now and schedule a recurring daily appointment with yourself to complete your morning success rituals. This will likely be the first hour or so after waking, or it may be the first hour at your office. *Do it now.*

- Make a list of the daily tasks that would significantly advance your business if they were to become habitual. *Do it now.*

- Share this daily task list with a trusted friend or colleague. *Do it now.*

Your 8-Step Dream Business Plan: In Summary

Step 1: The 10-Year Dream

Step 2: The 5-Year Vision

Step 3: The 3-Year Plan

Step 4: The 1-Year Goal

Step 5: The 3-Month Review

Step 6: The 1-Month Schedule

Step 7: The 1-Week Focus

Step 8: The 1-Day Task List

Conclusion

Venturing into business for oneself, particularly after having been an employee for many years, is not for the feint of heart. It requires dedication and a strong business mindset. Sailing a ship through the rough waters of self-employment is a challenge for any captain of business. The 8 Step Dream Business Plan is meant as a guide to help navigate those stormy seas. If fully implemented, it will help a new business owner to know when to trim the sails, batten down the hatches, and drop anchor. It is also meant as a beacon of optimism and progress. It is like a lighthouse but can be referred to again and again to avoid the jagged rocks and the hidden sandbars. And if used with diligence, it can help you catch the full wind of your growing enterprise, cutting through the waves and speeding toward your business dream.

If you follow through with each step in the 8-Step Dream Business Plan, you will not only be running an efficient and organized business, but you will be able to do so with the reassurance that everything has been thoroughly planned out and executed. I hope that you enjoy the process of up-leveling your business.